Majestic Lions:
A Stress-Relieving Coloring Book for Adults

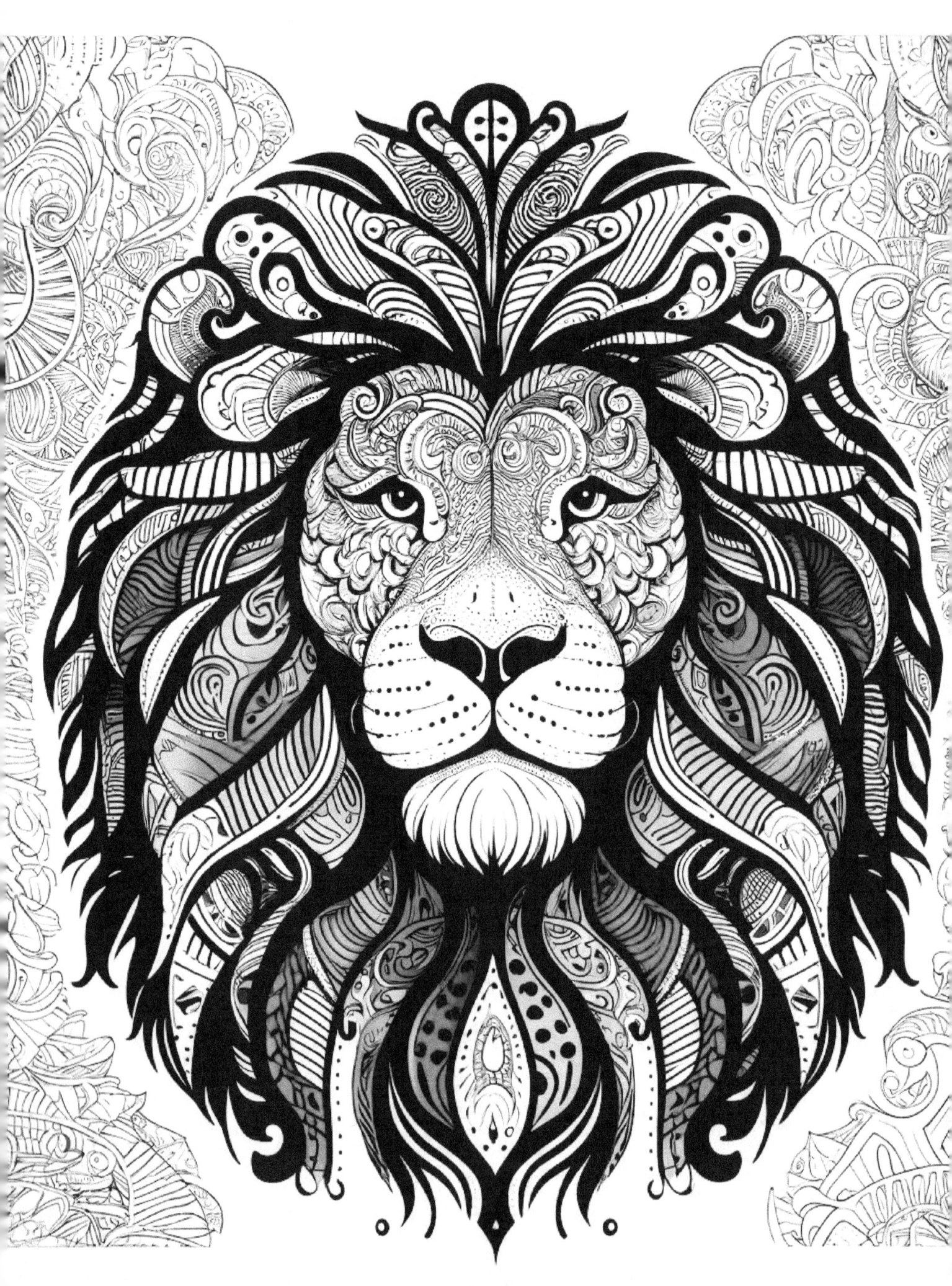

Welcome to "Majestic Lions: A Stress-Relieving Coloring Book for Adults." In this book, you will embark on a journey through the regal world of lions. Each page is filled with intricately detailed illustrations showcasing the majesty and beauty of these magnificent creatures.

Coloring is more than just a hobby; it's a way to unwind, relax, and find inner peace. As you immerse yourself in these intricate designs, let the power and grace of the lion inspire you. Feel the stress of daily life fade away as you focus on bringing each lion to life with your choice of colors.

Whether you are an experienced colorist or new to this creative outlet, "Majestic Lions" offers a unique opportunity to explore your artistic side while enjoying the therapeutic benefits of coloring.

Grab your favorite coloring tools, find a quiet space, and let your creativity soar.

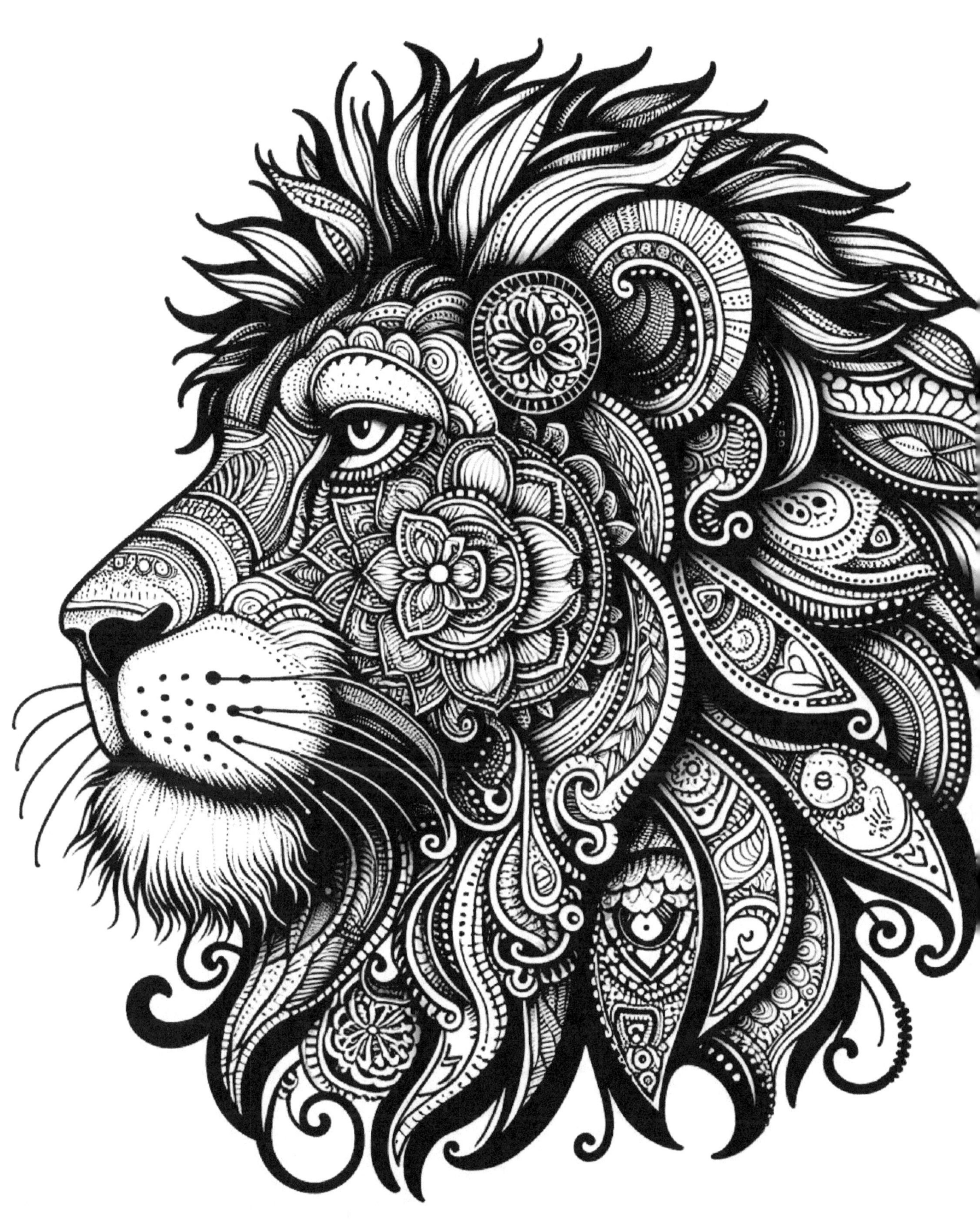

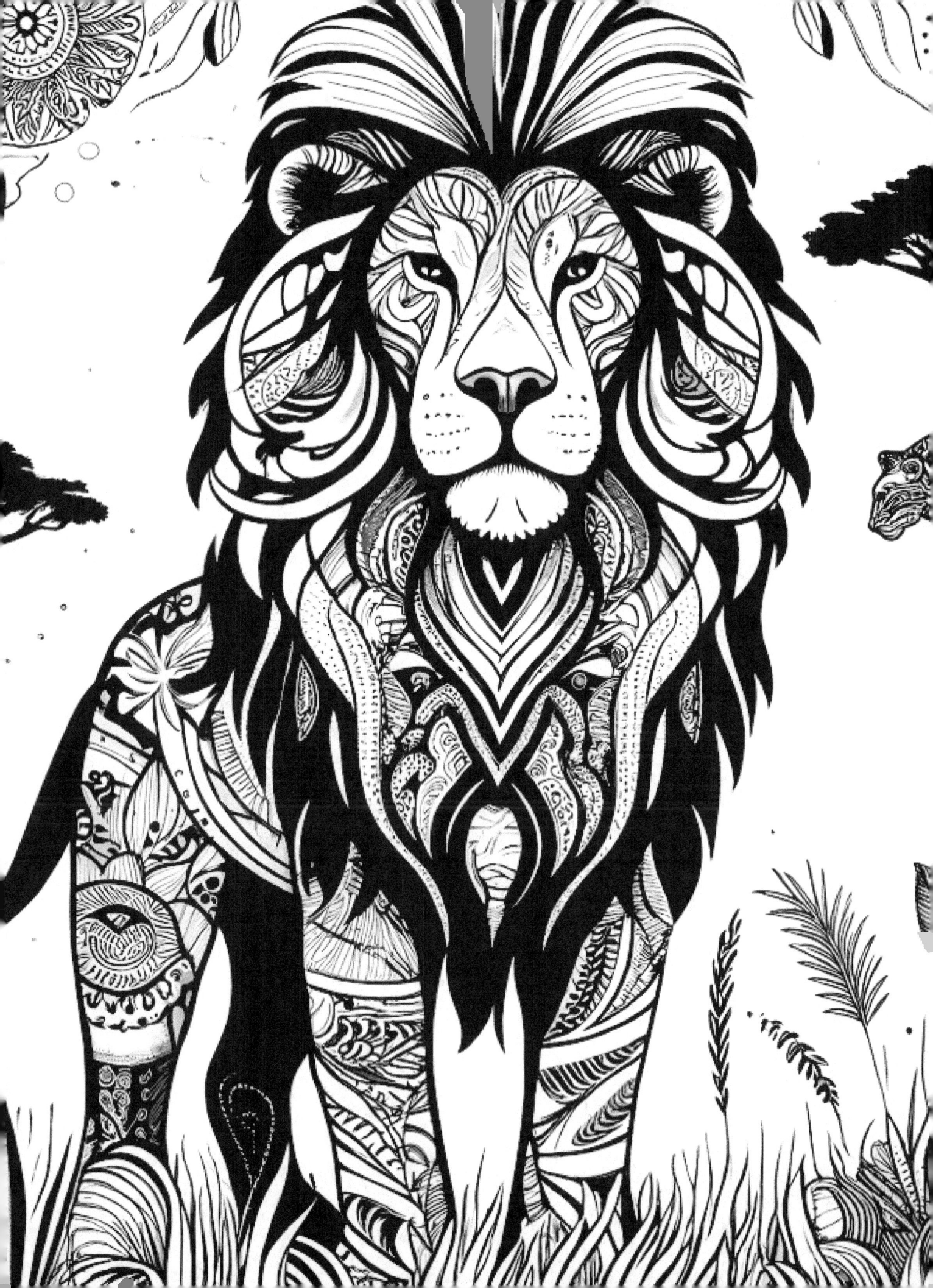

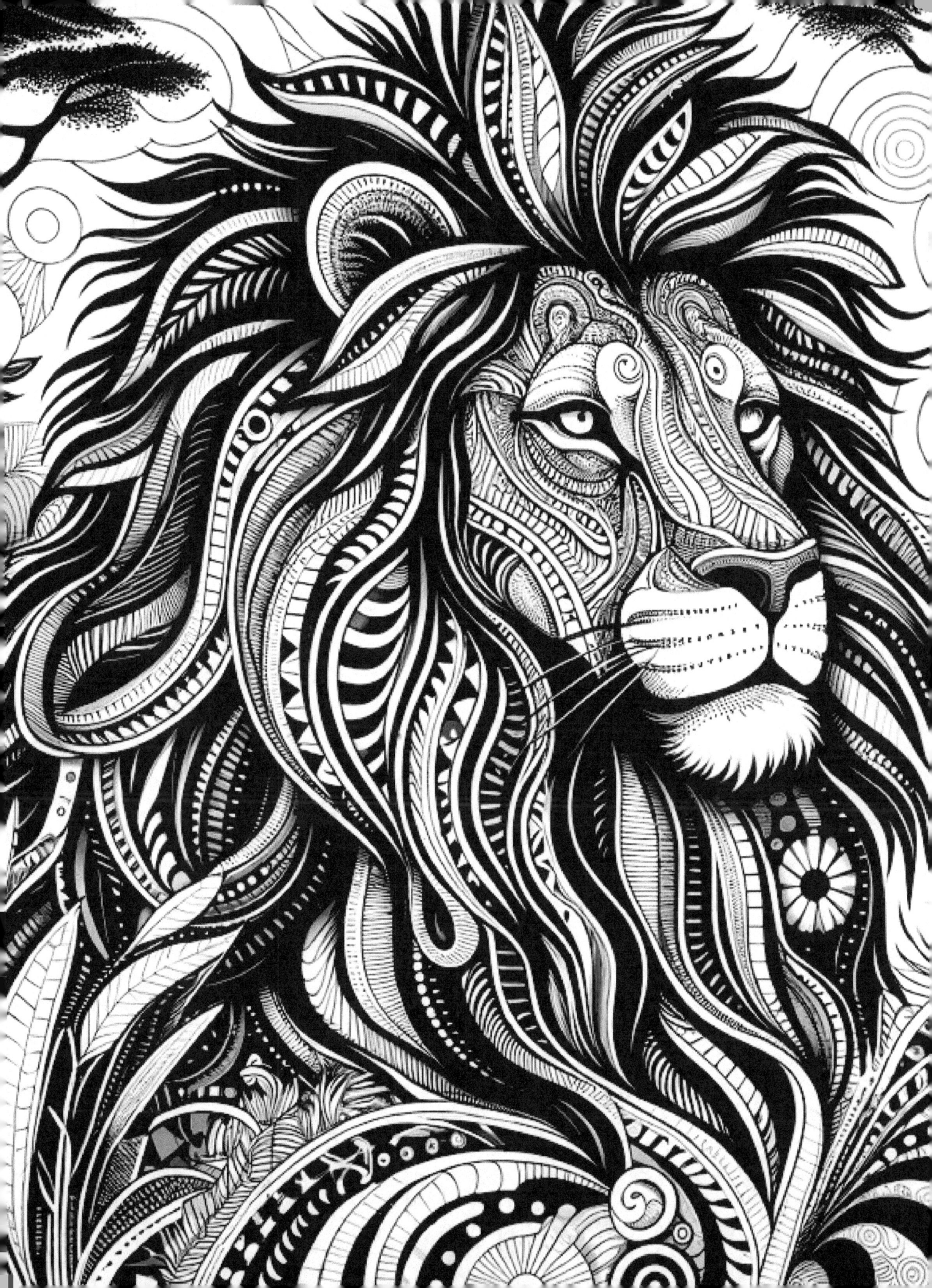

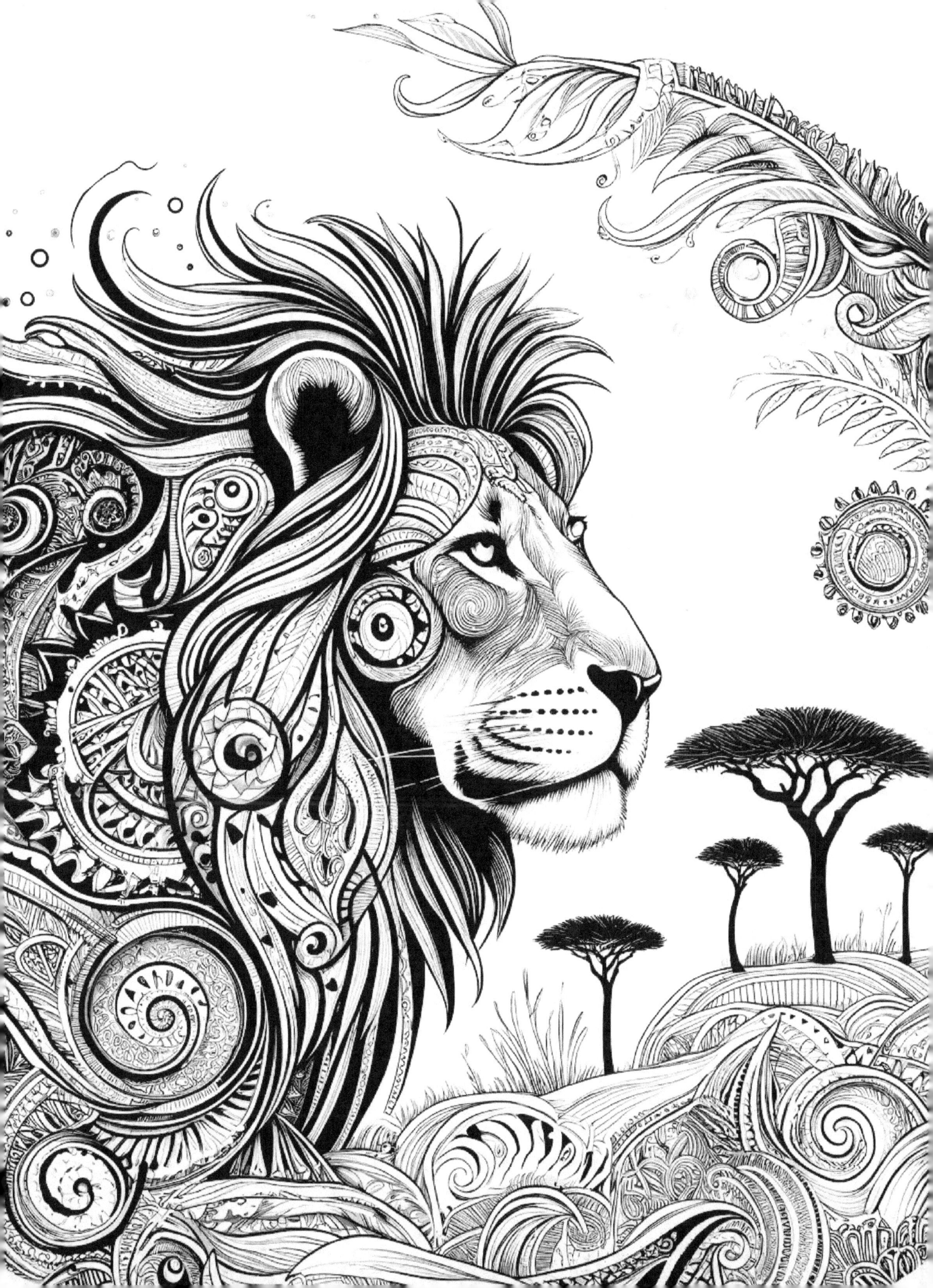

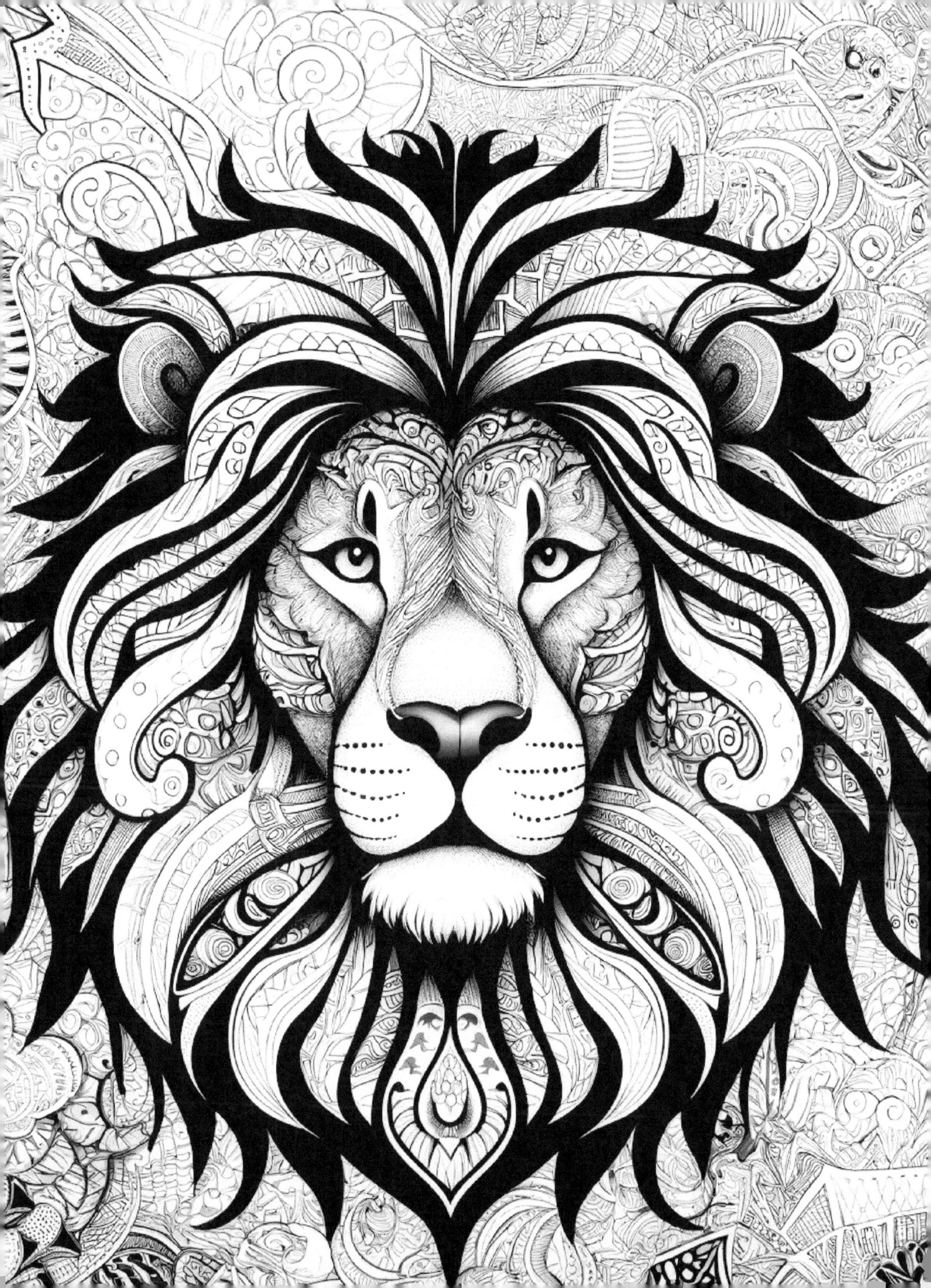

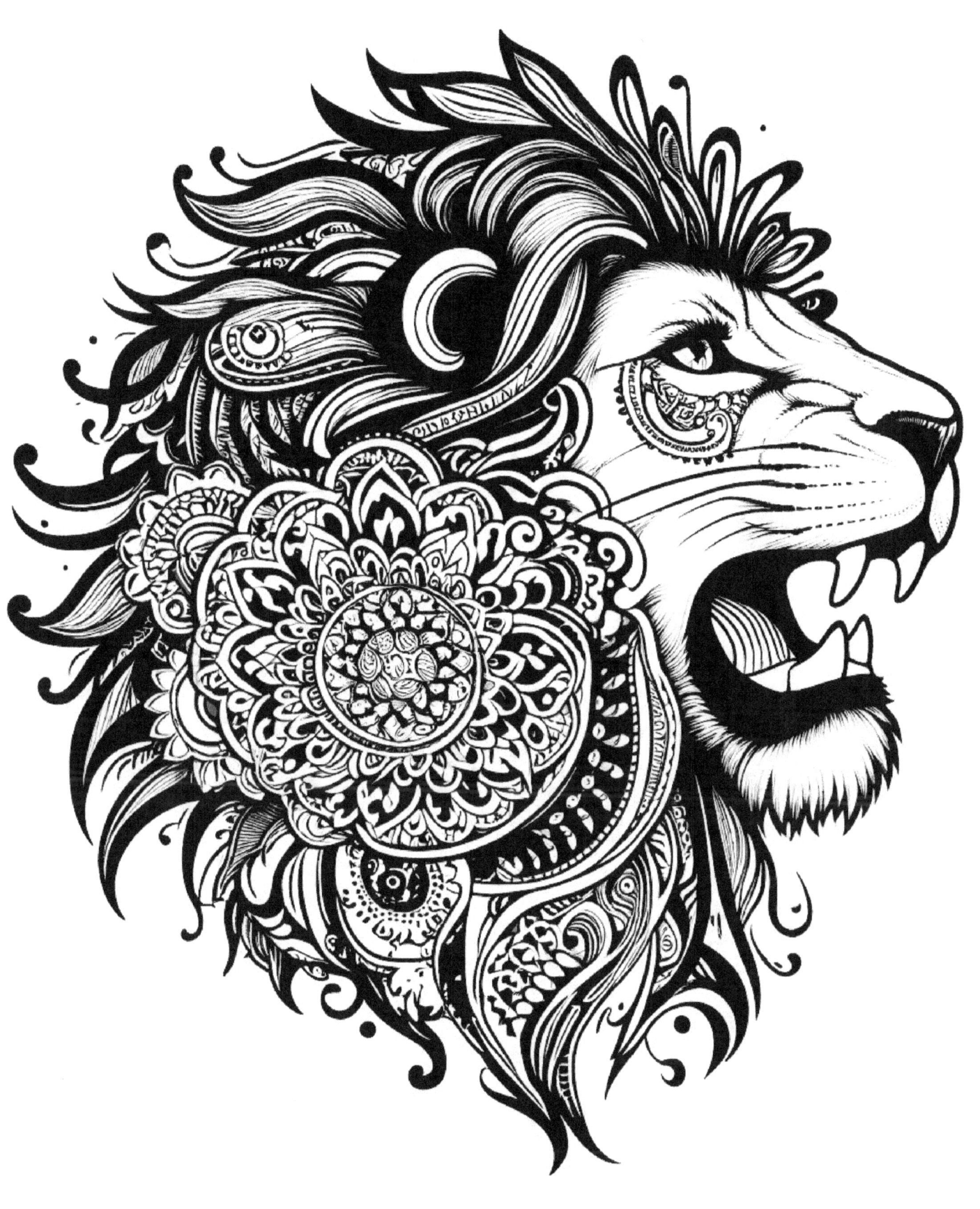

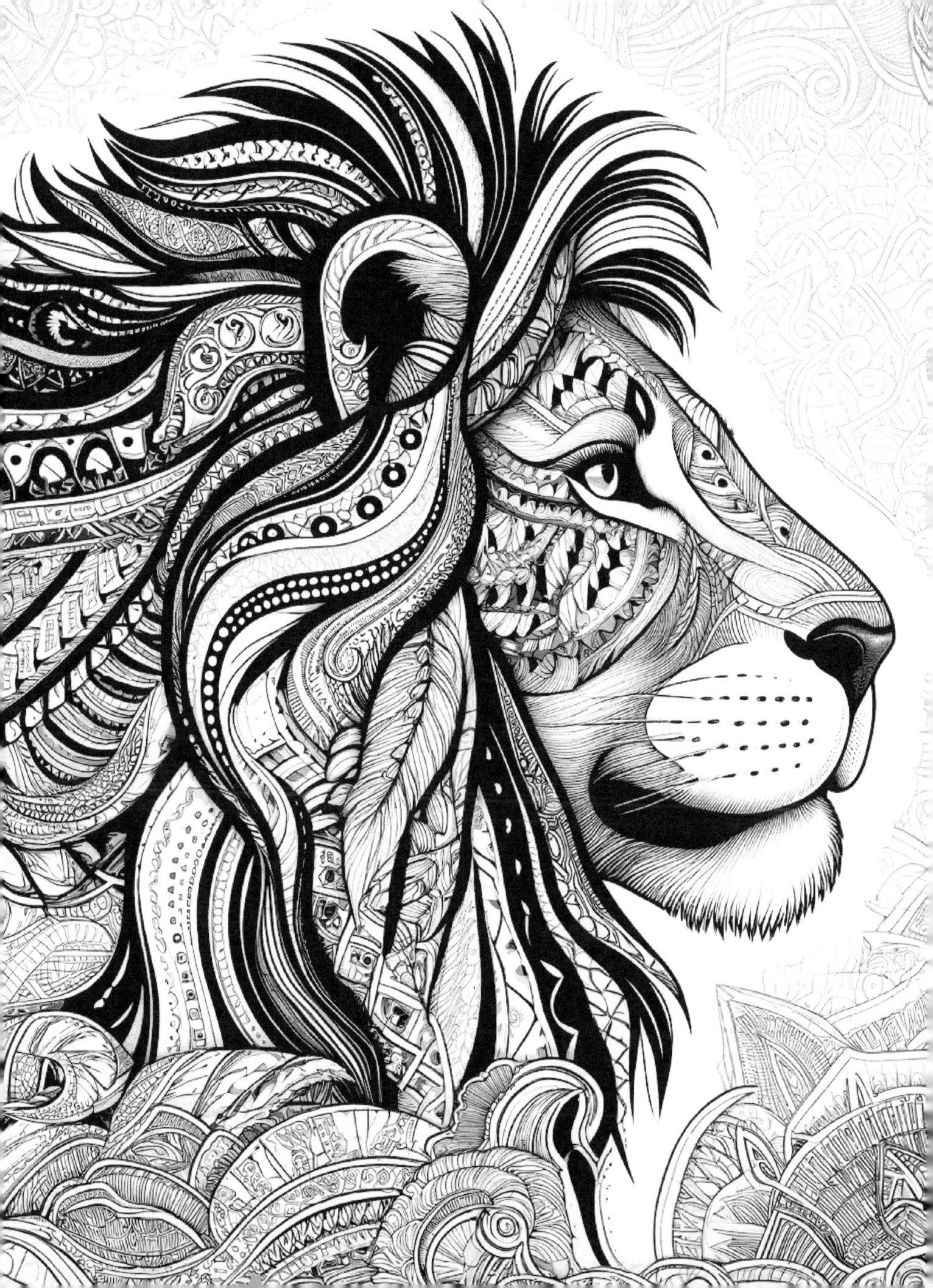

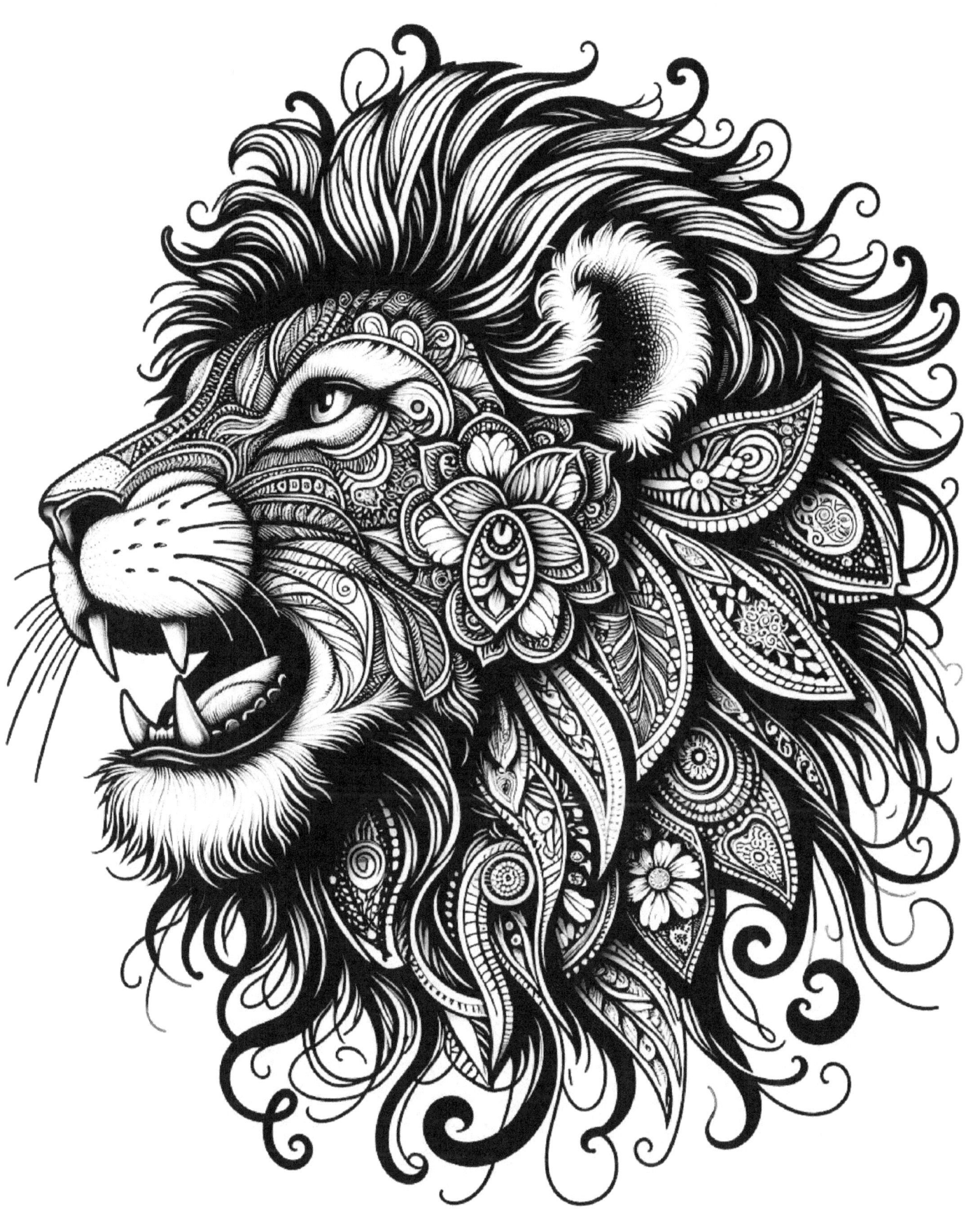

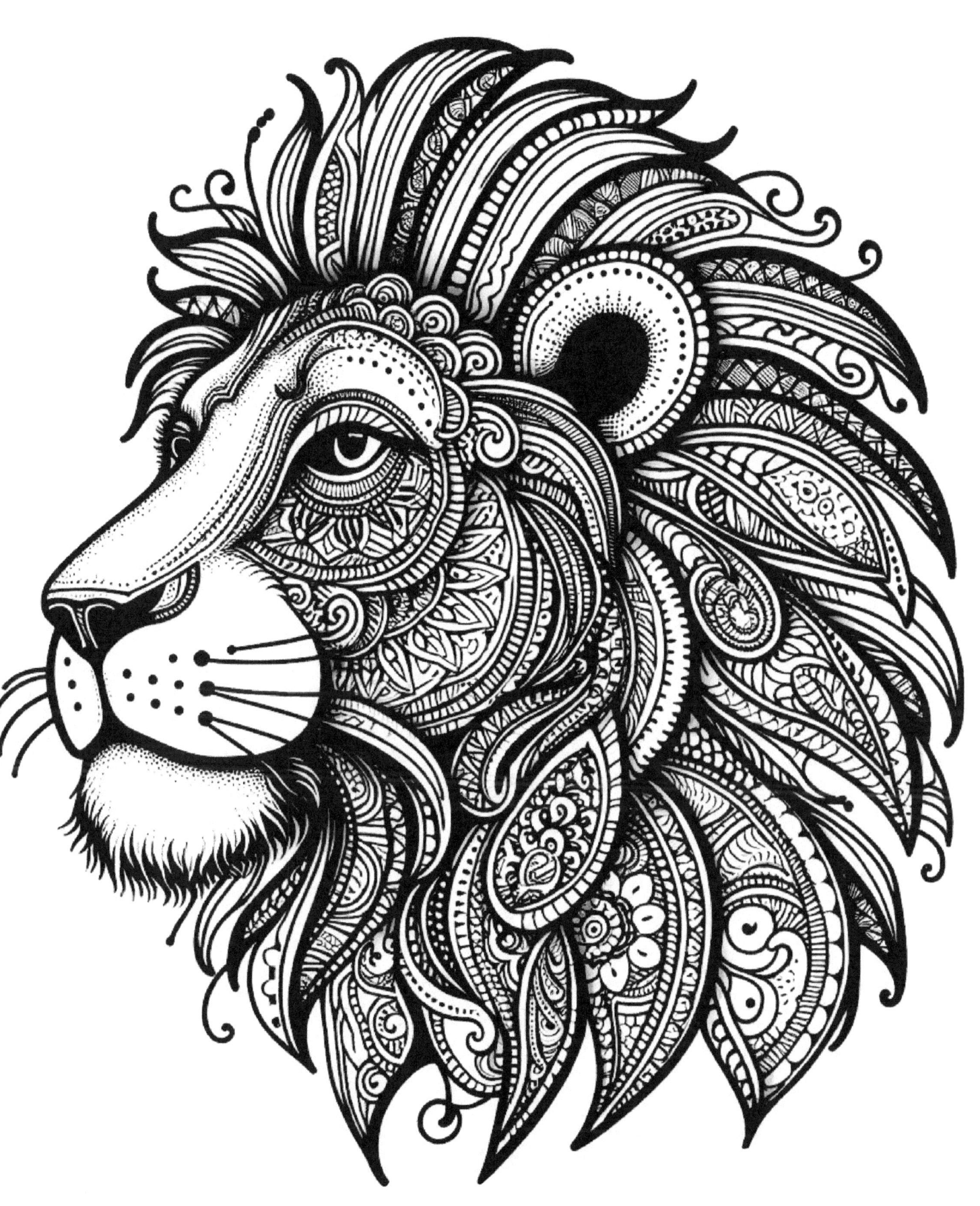

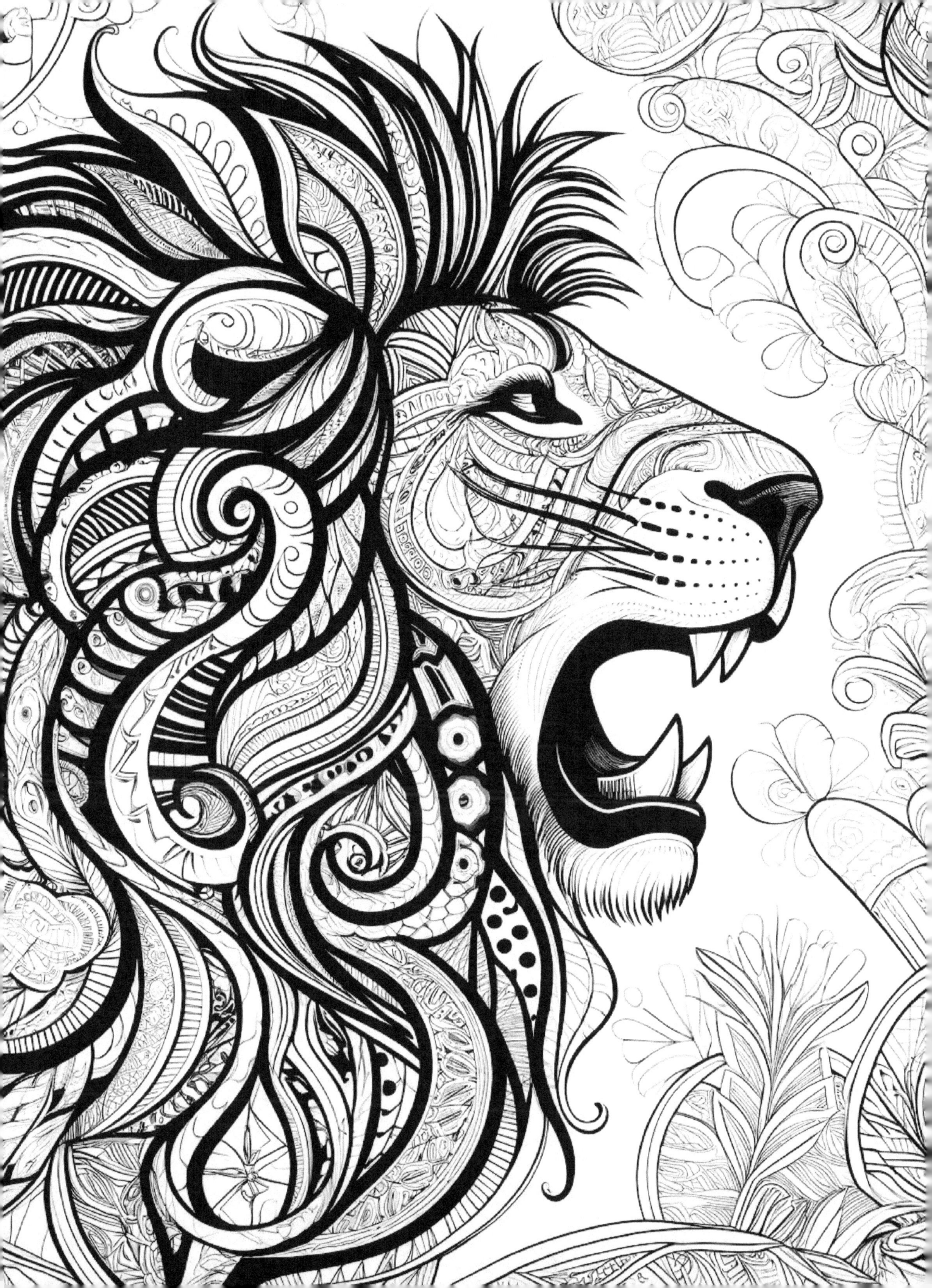

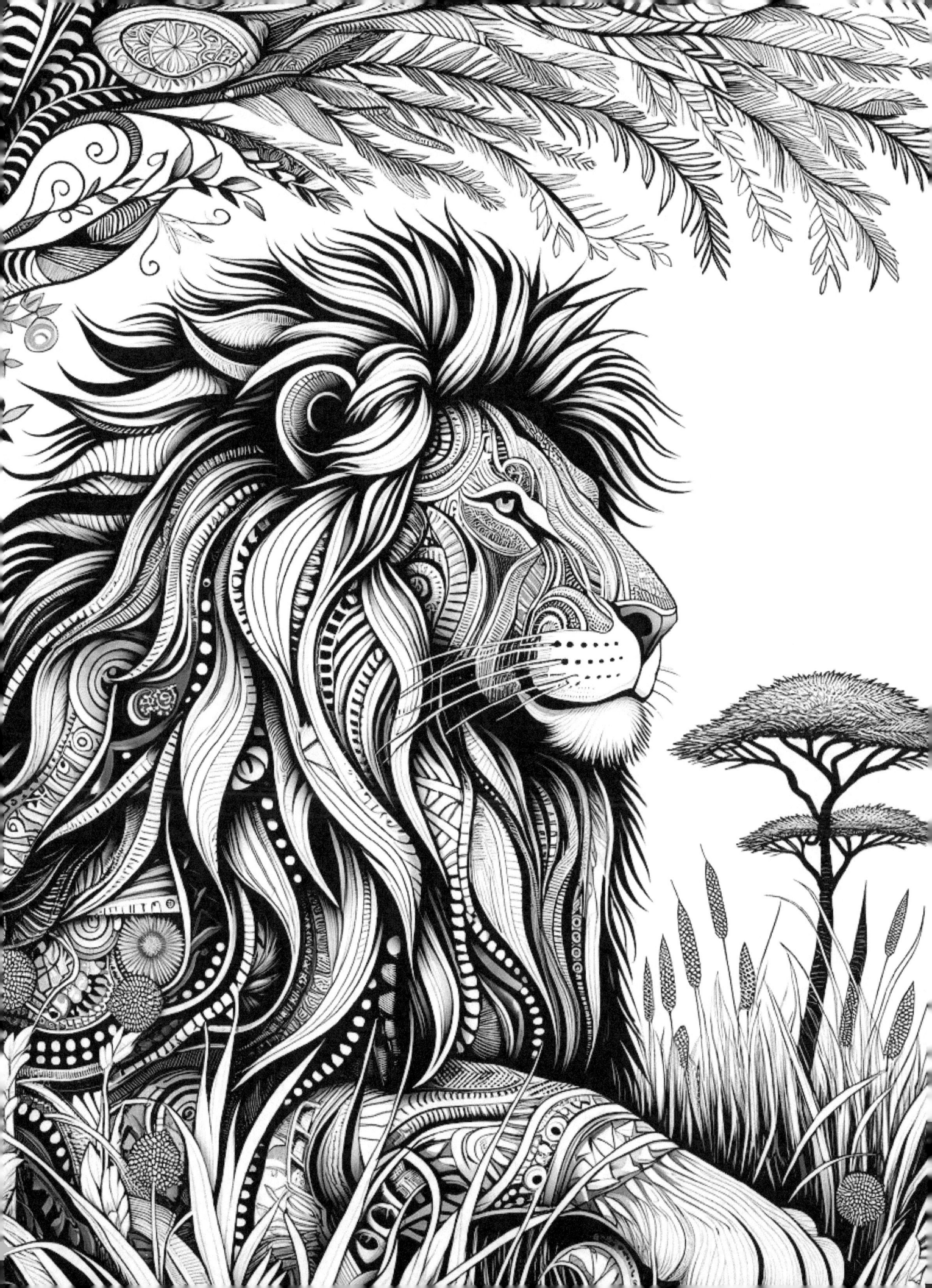

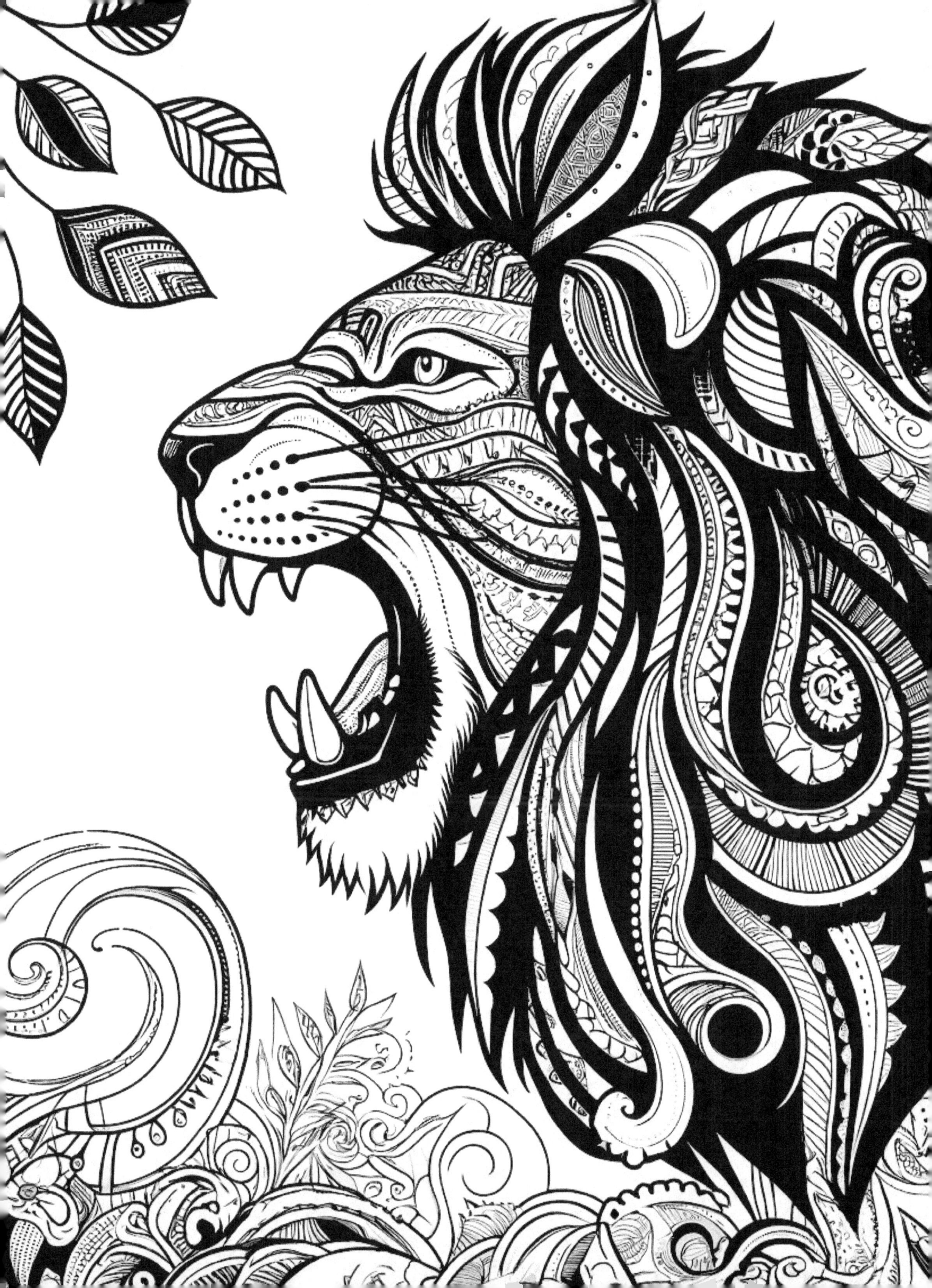

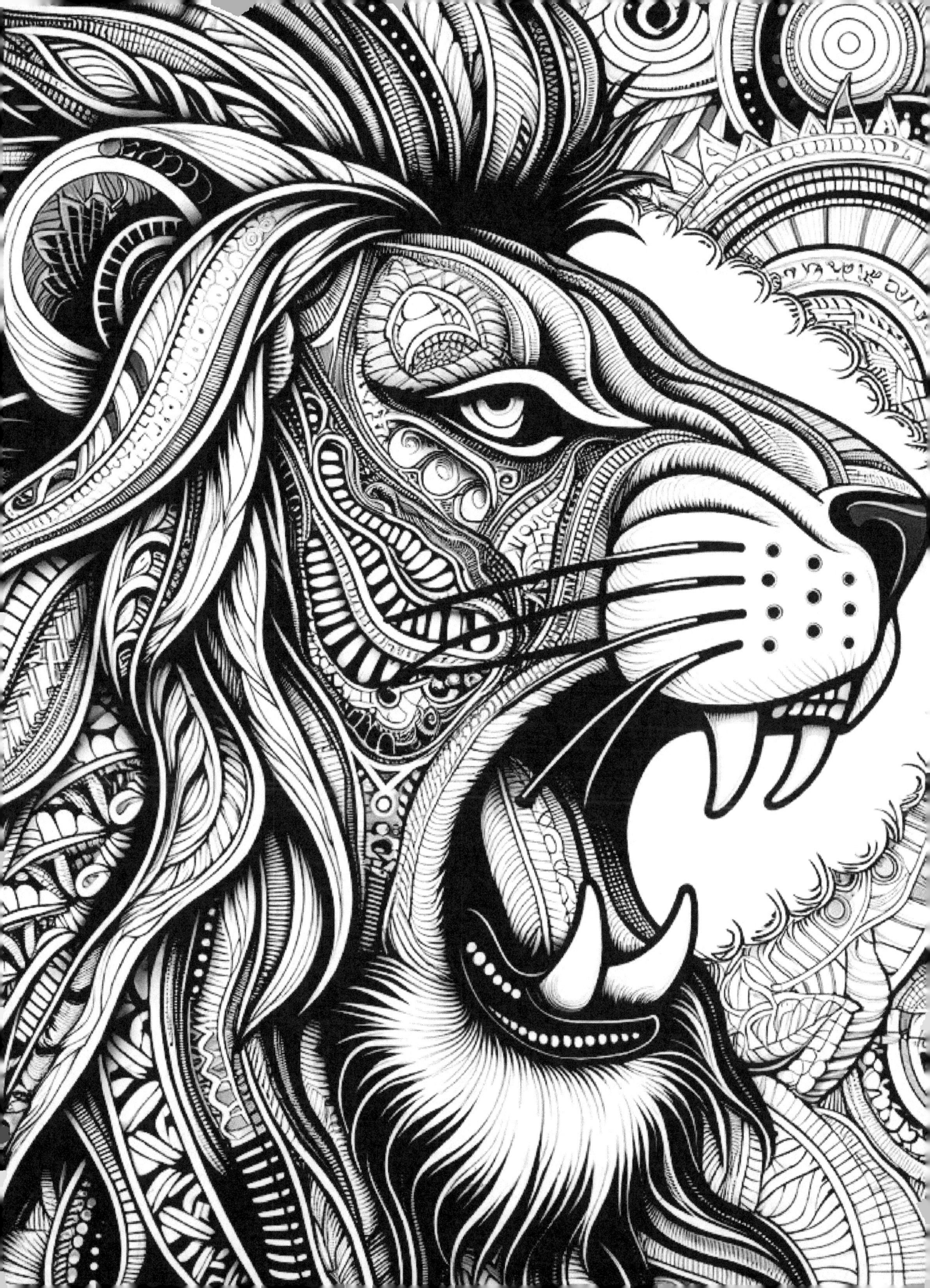

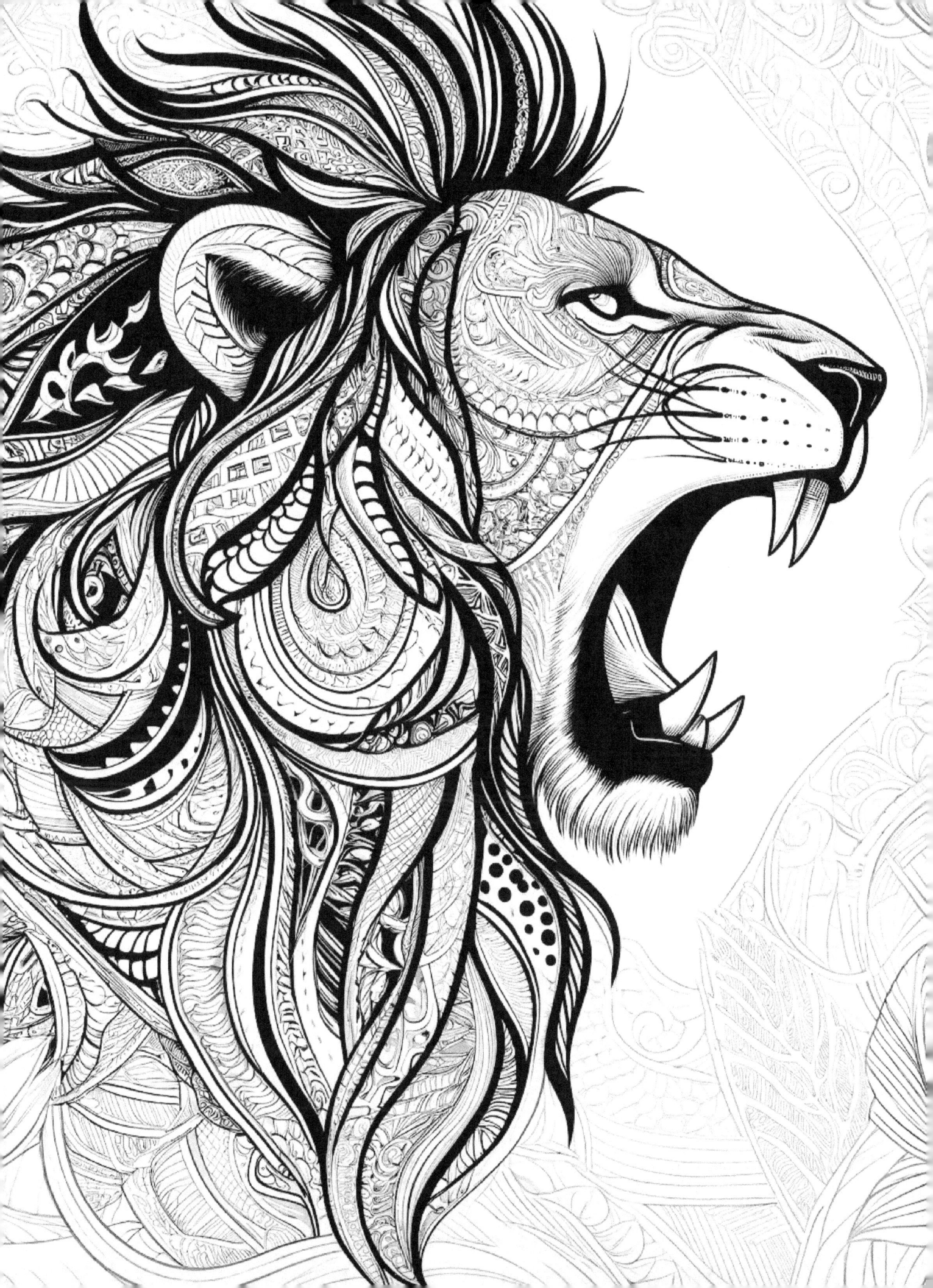

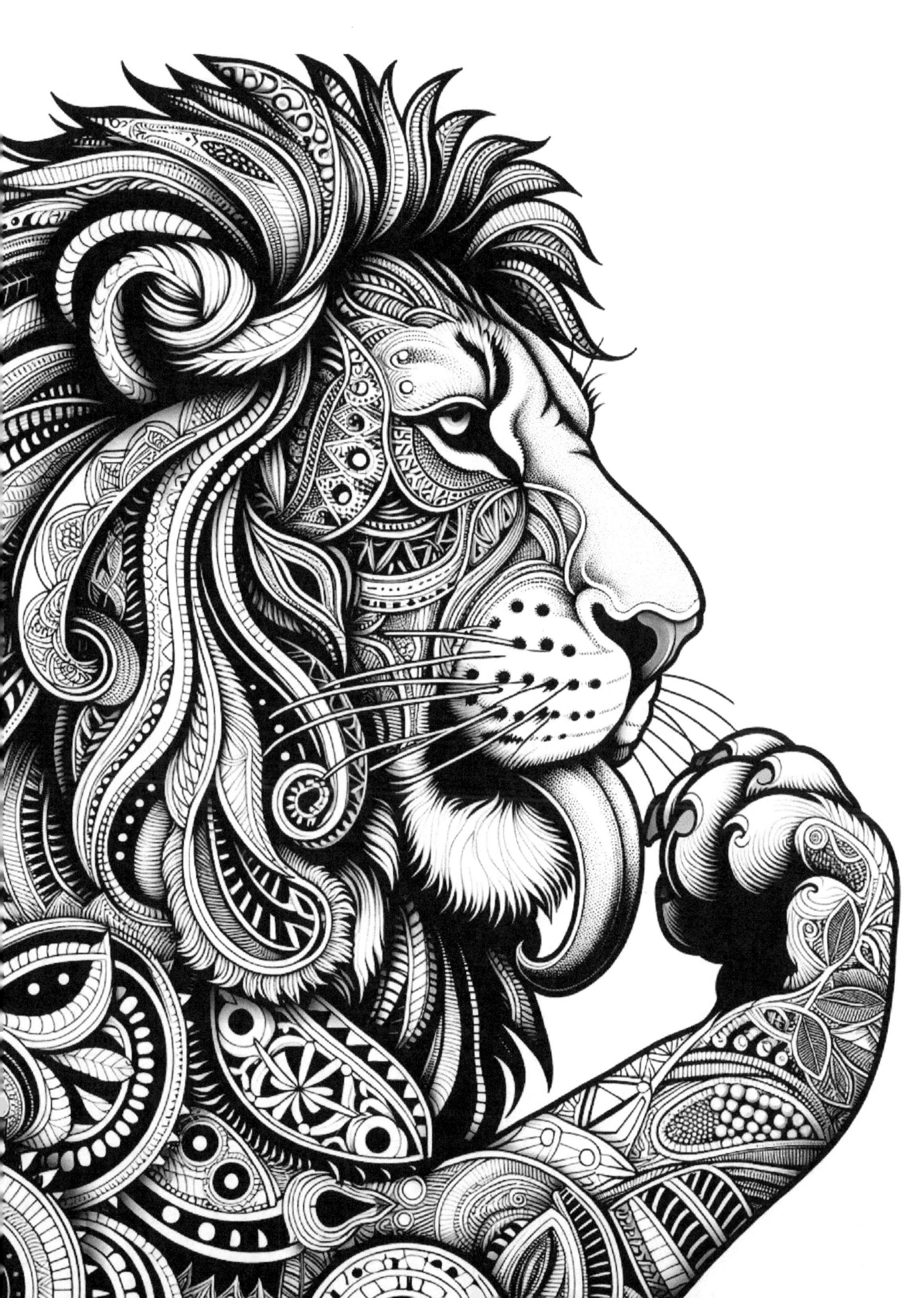

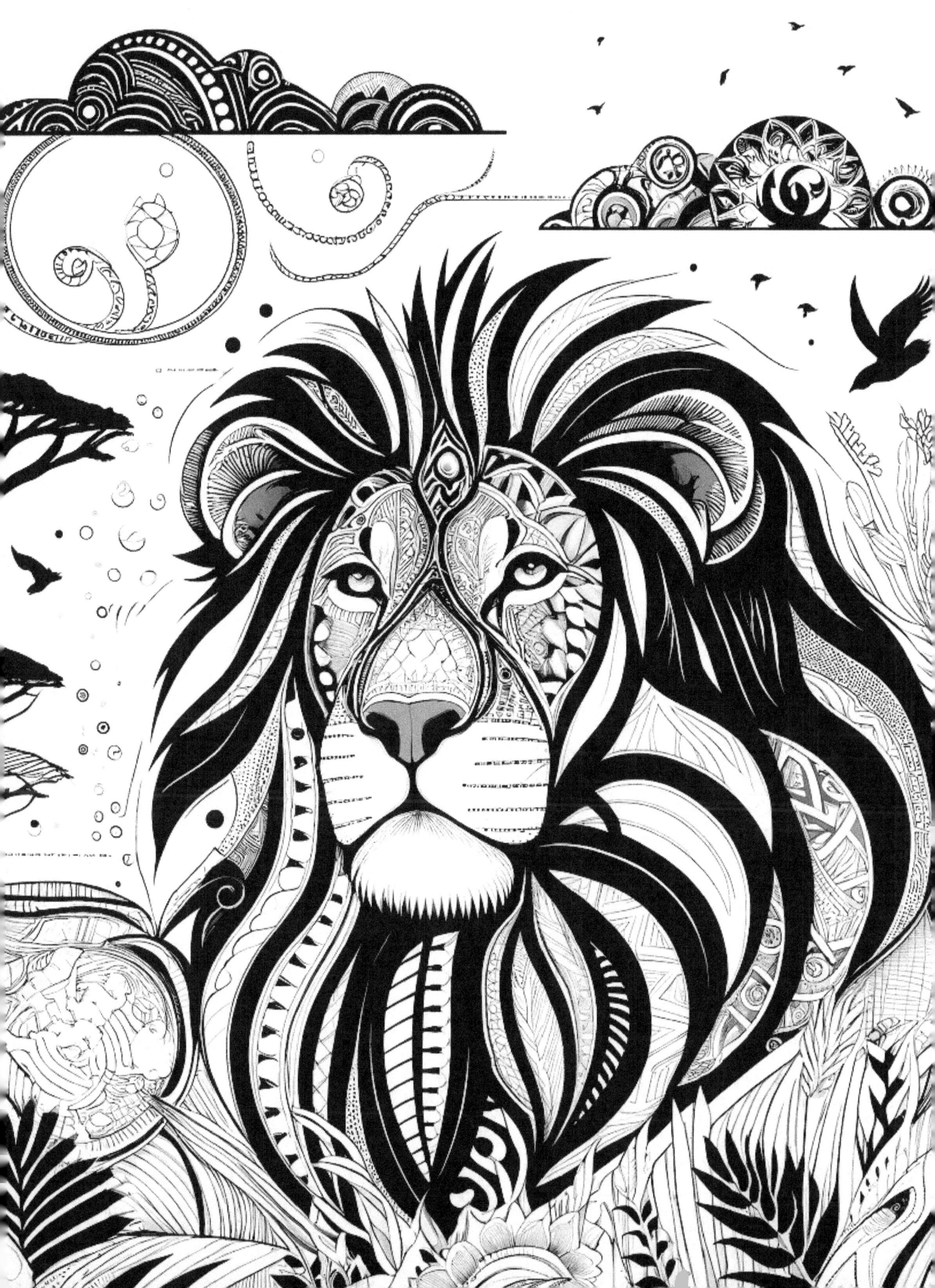

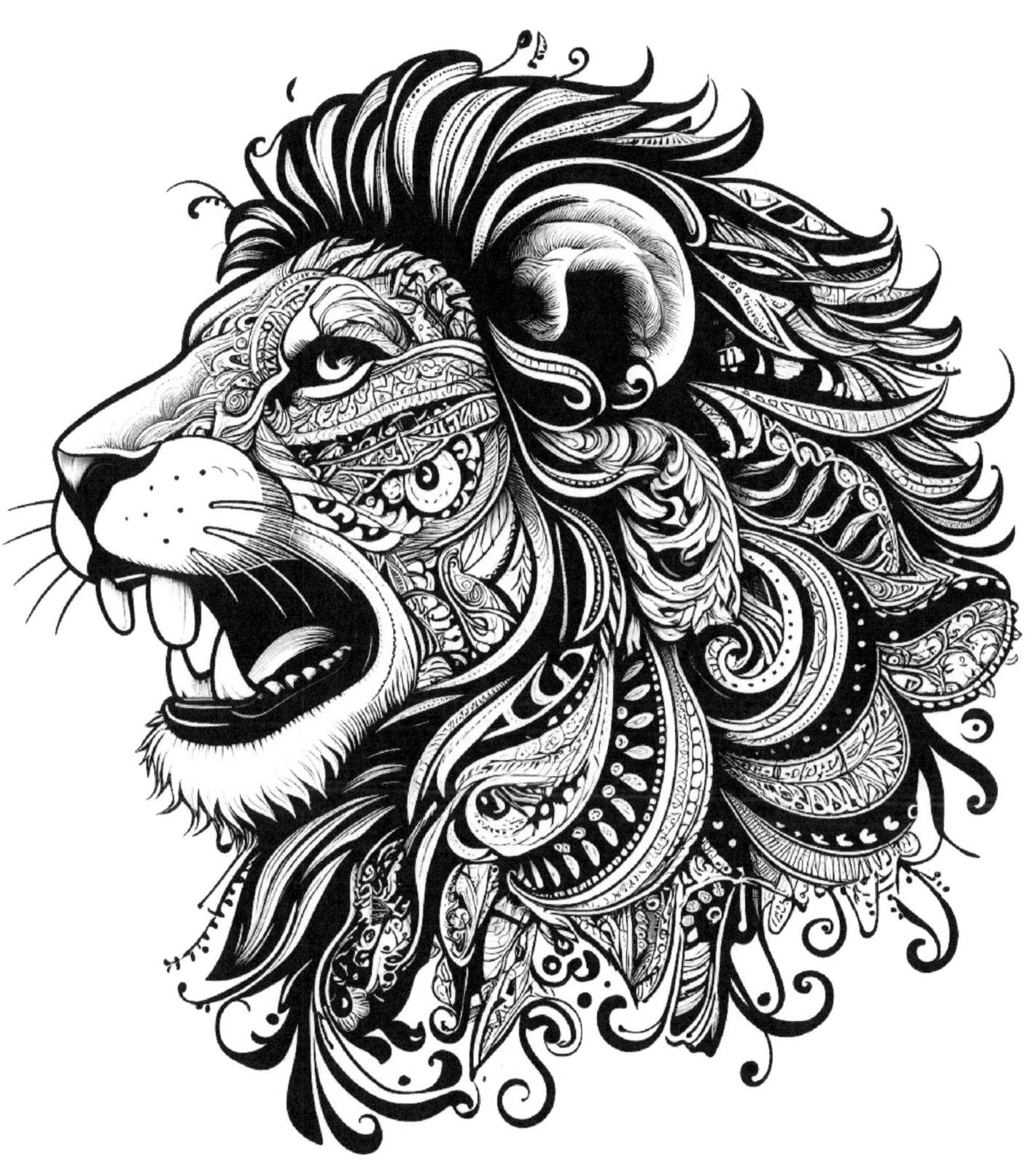

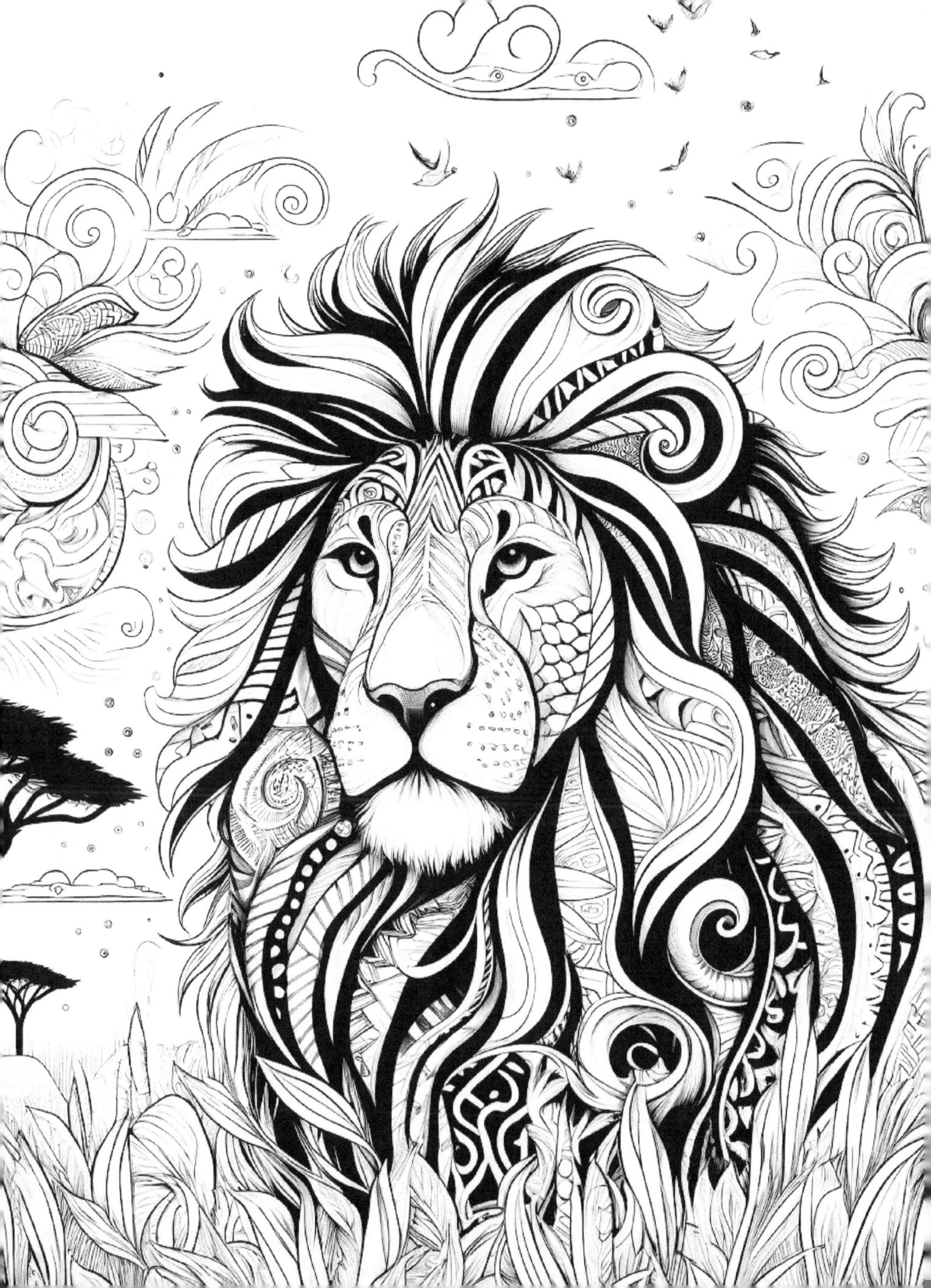

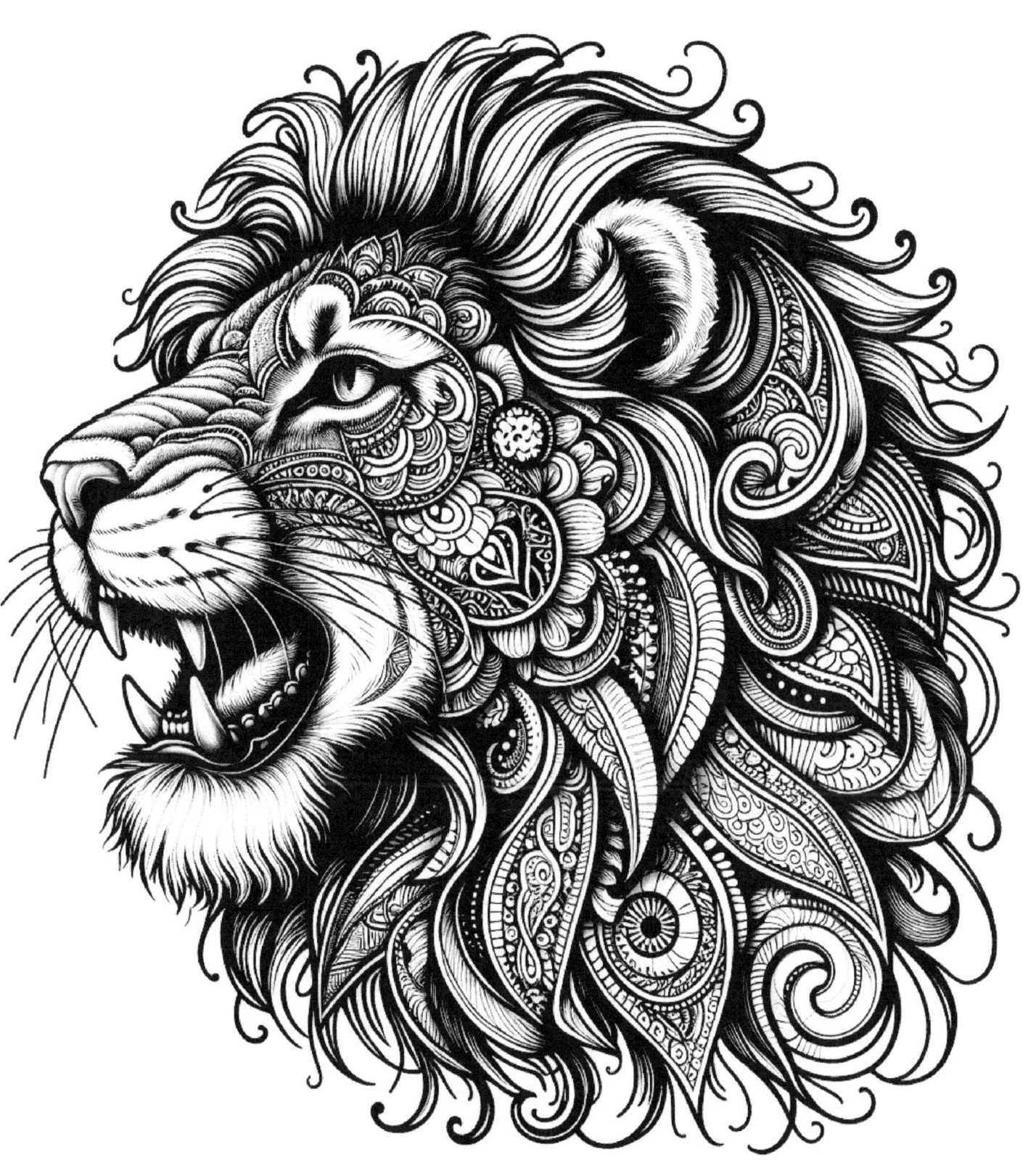

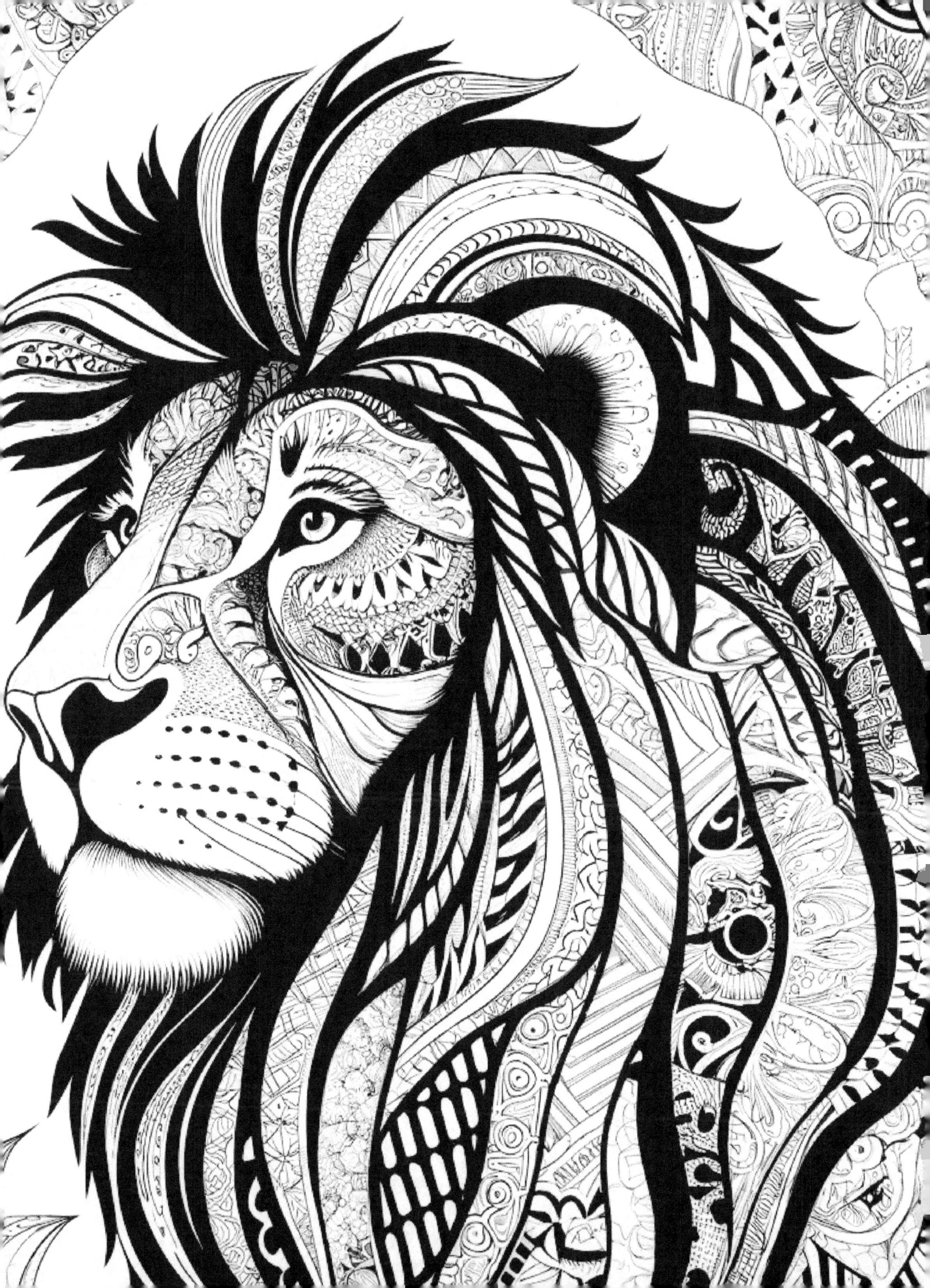

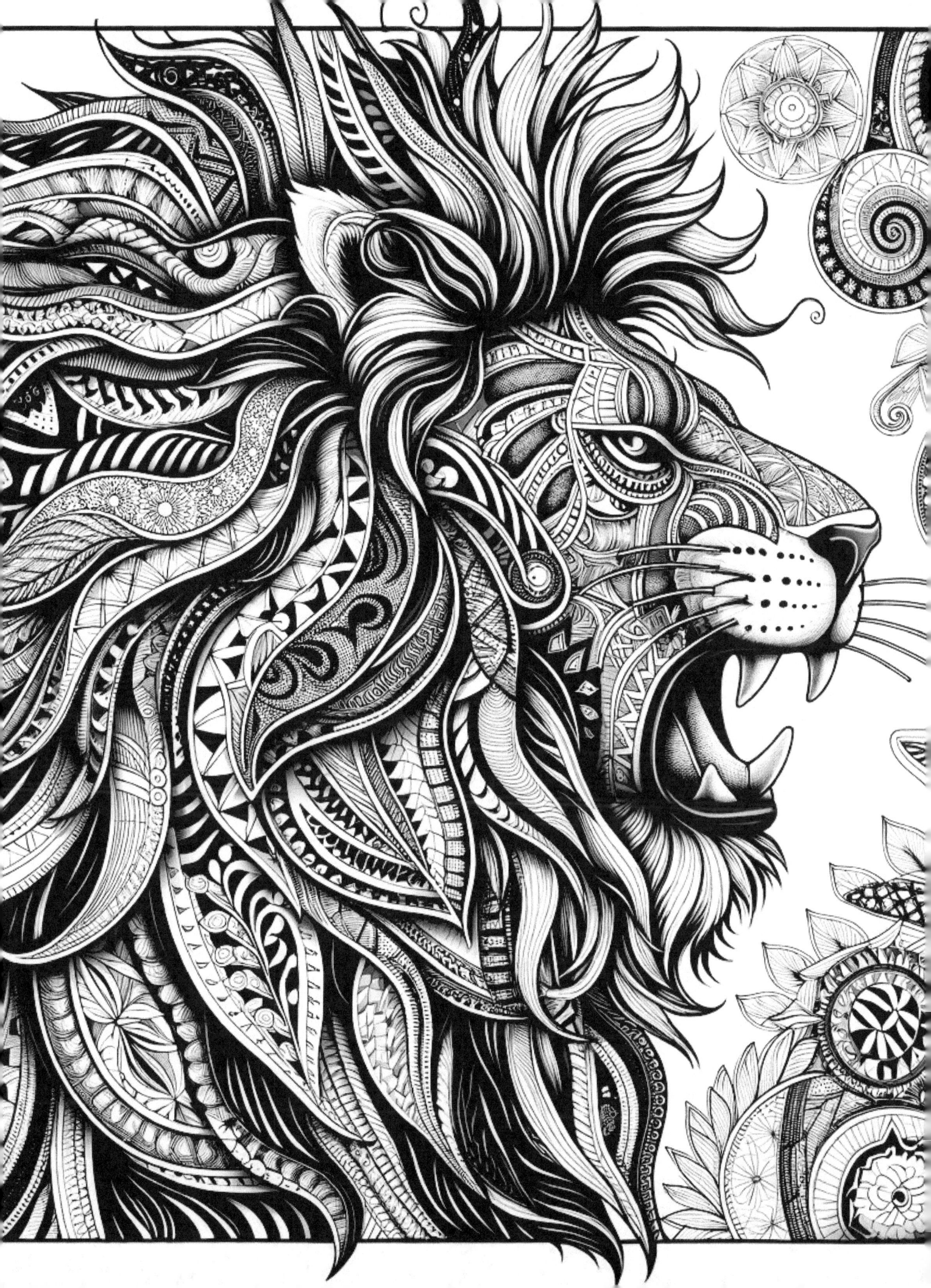

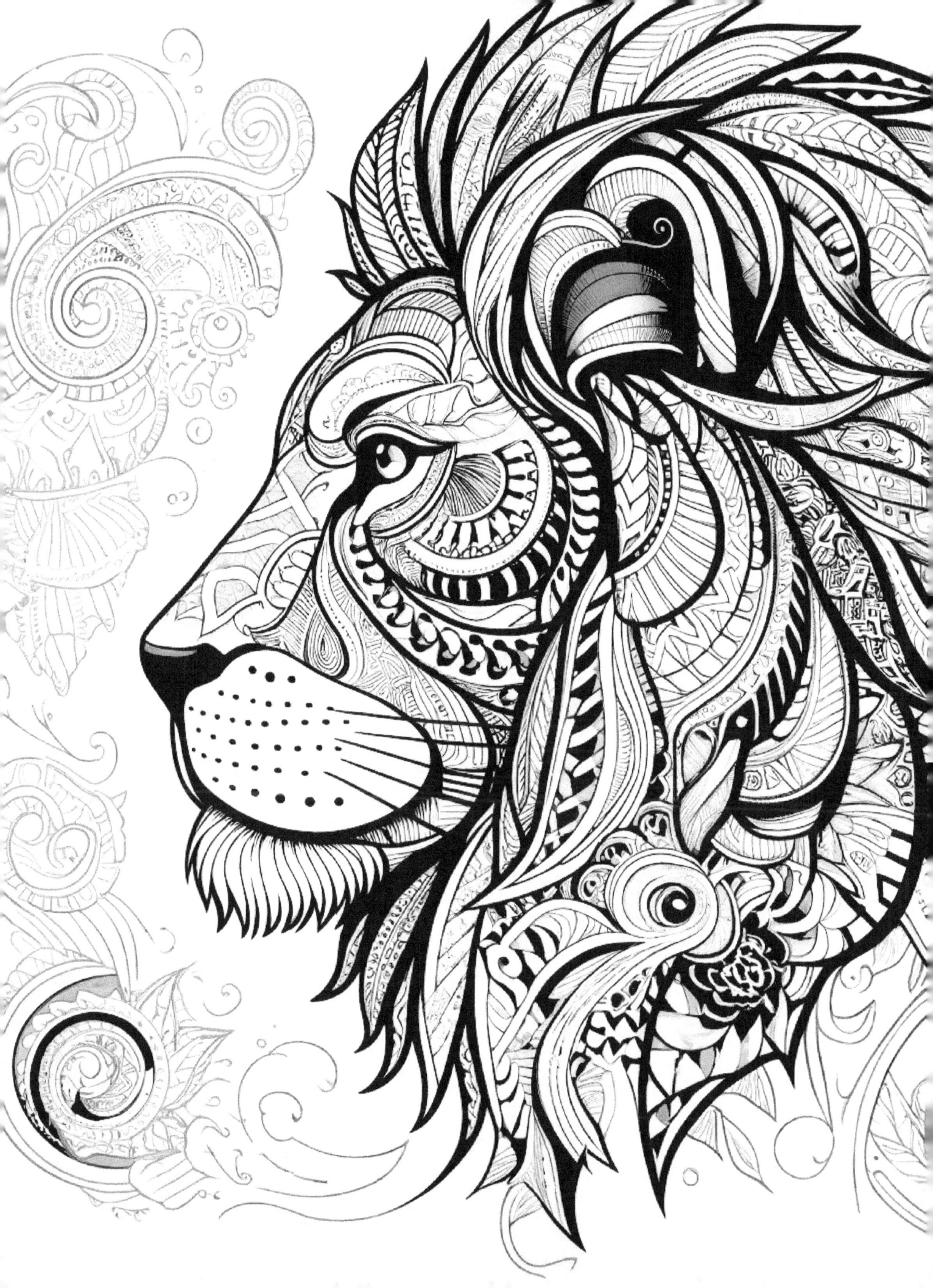

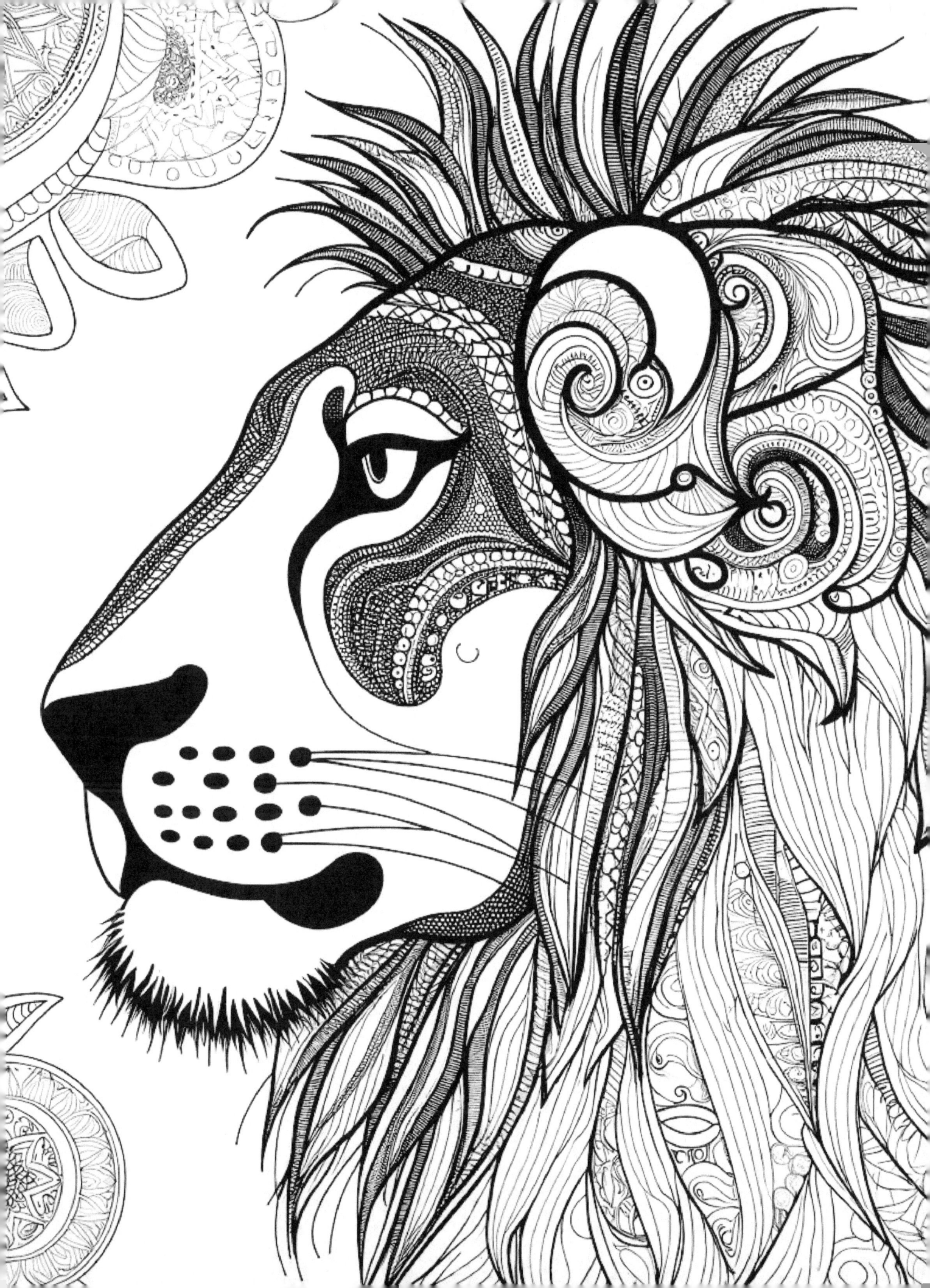

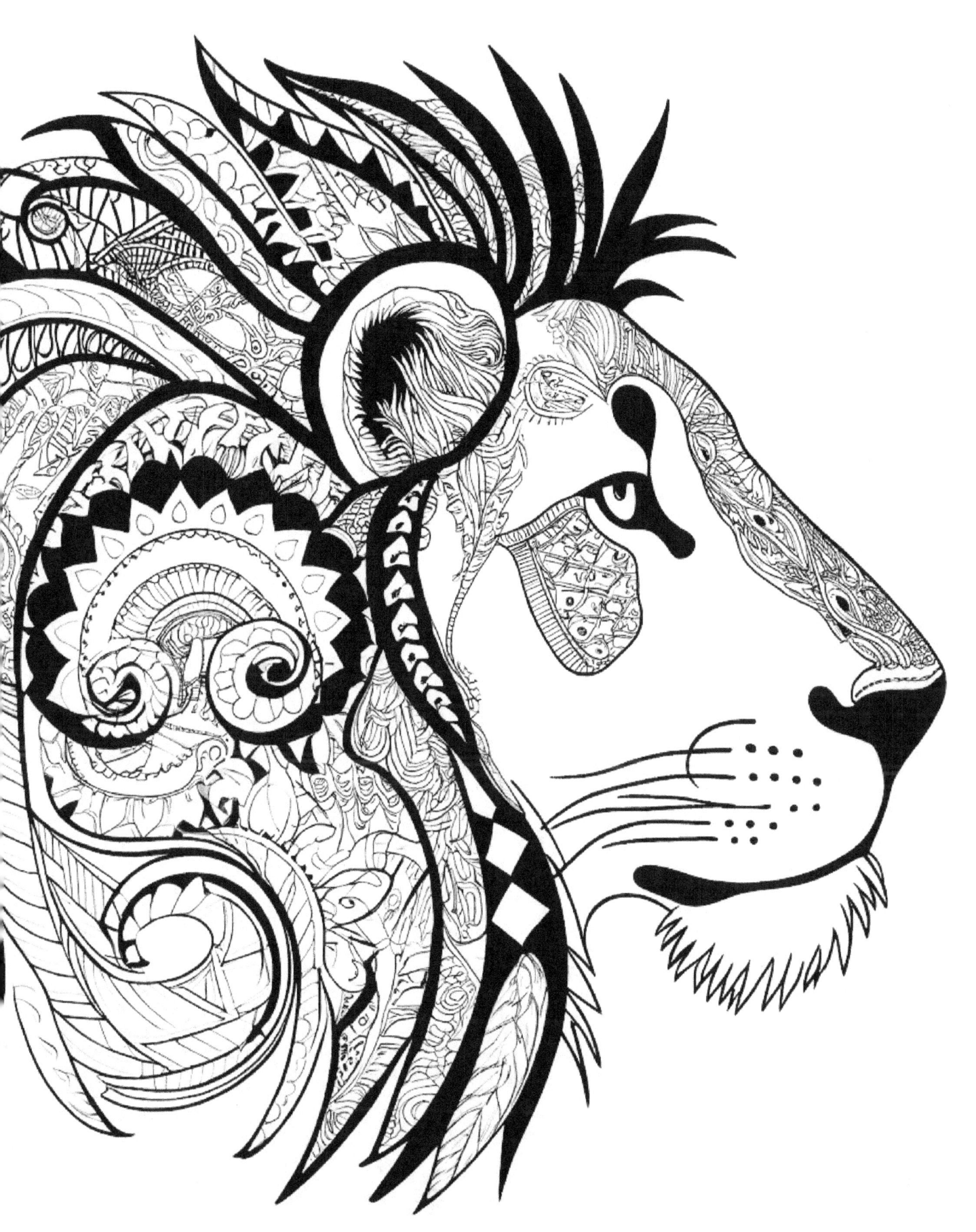

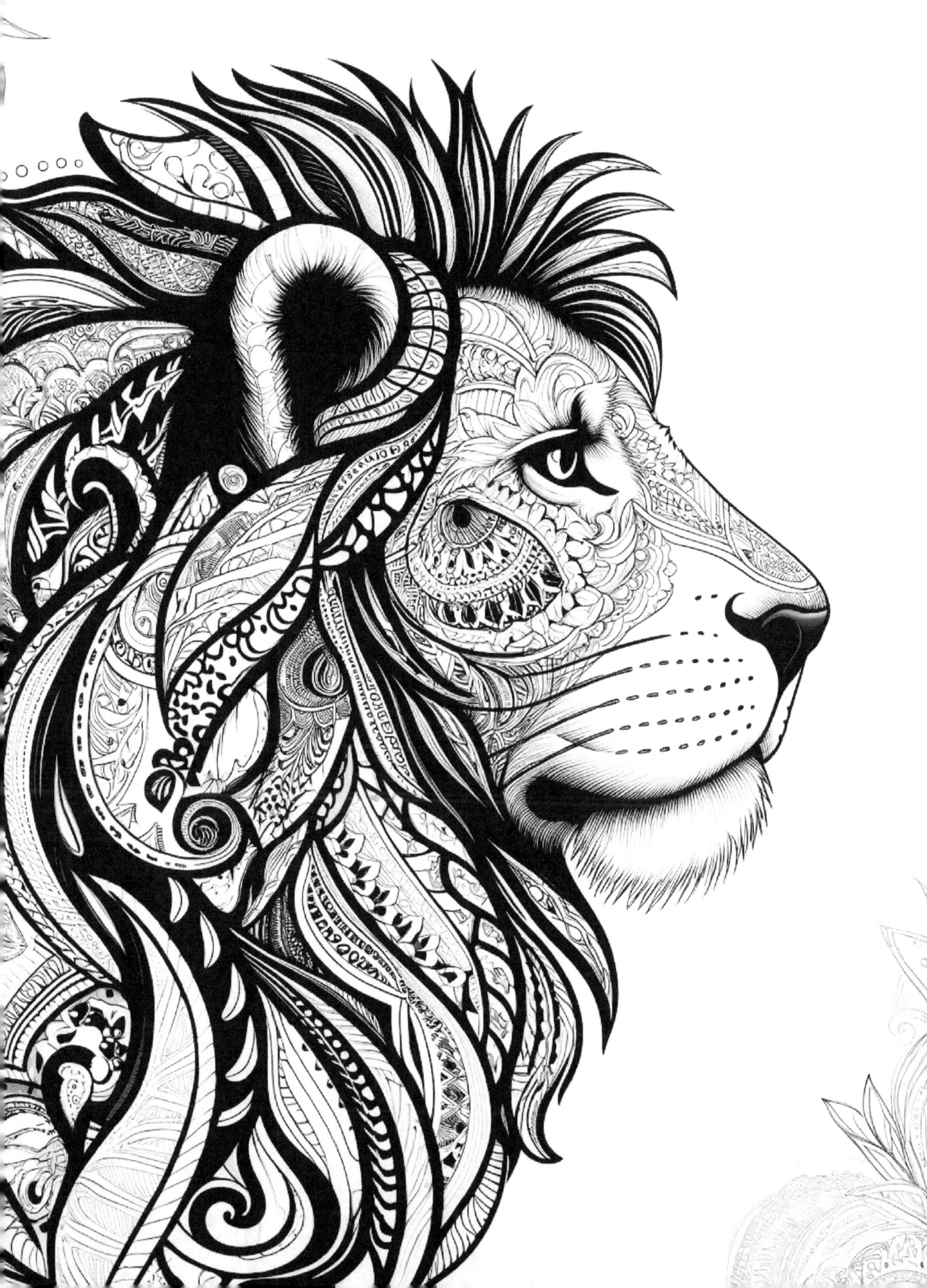

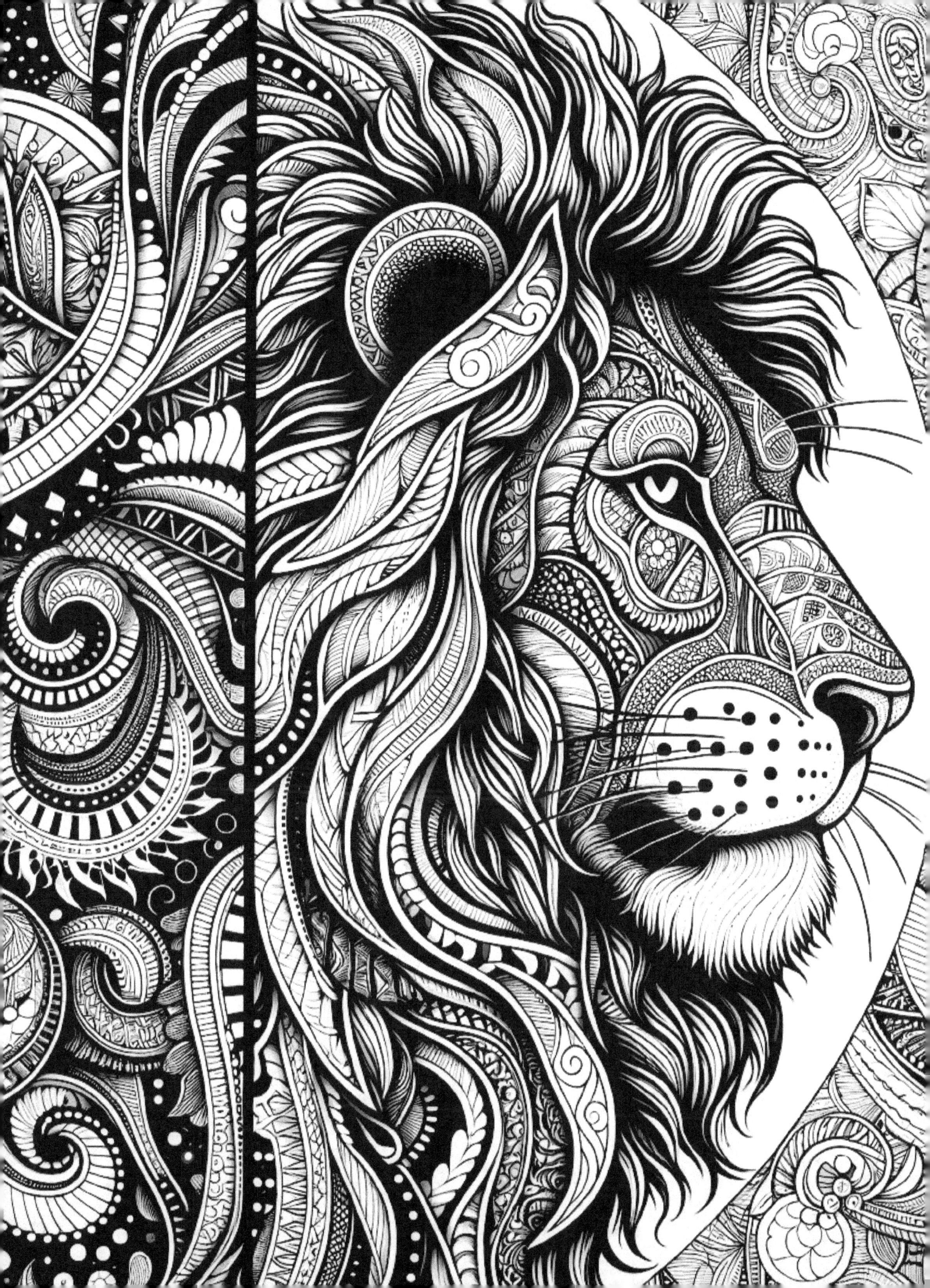

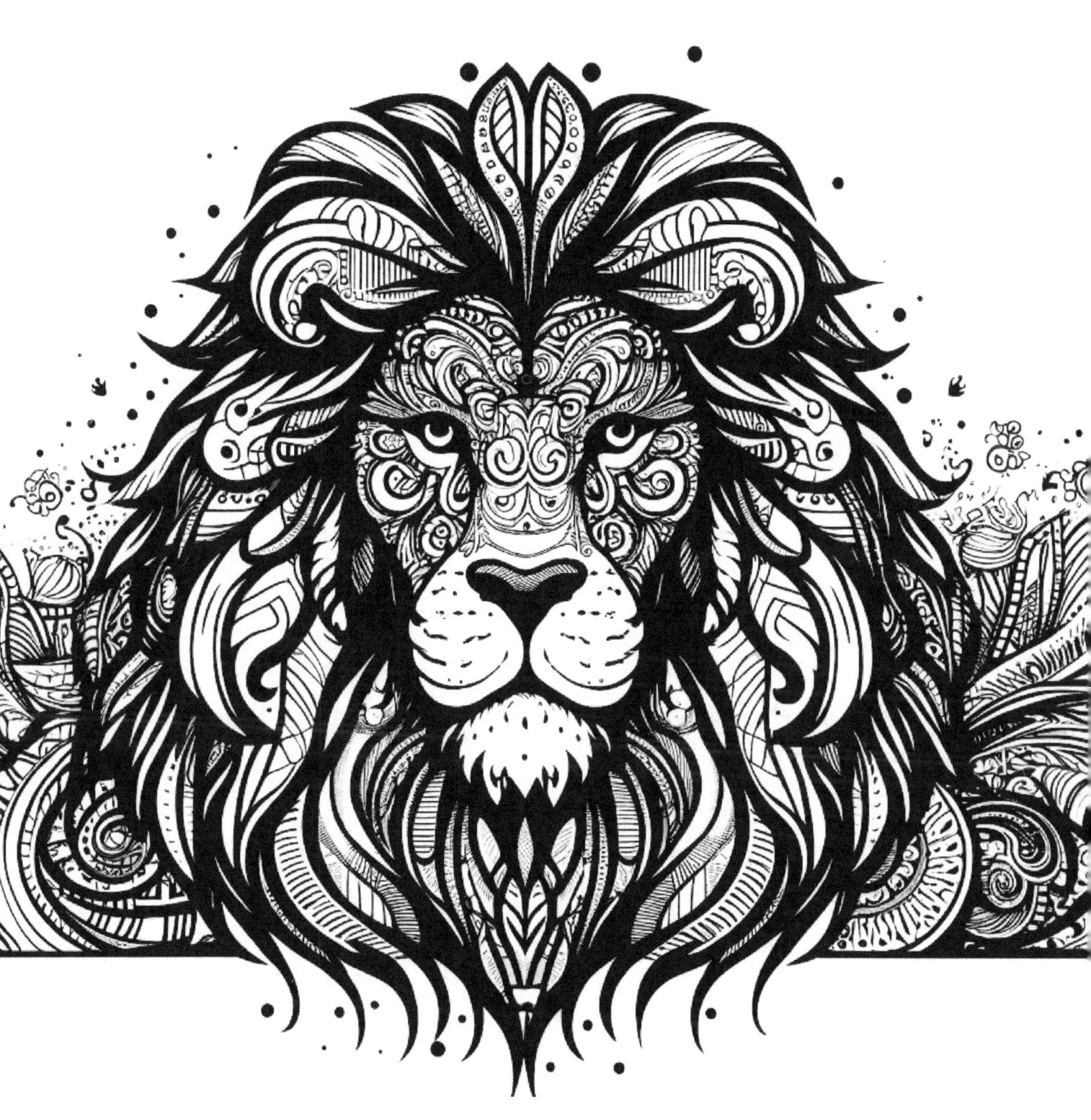

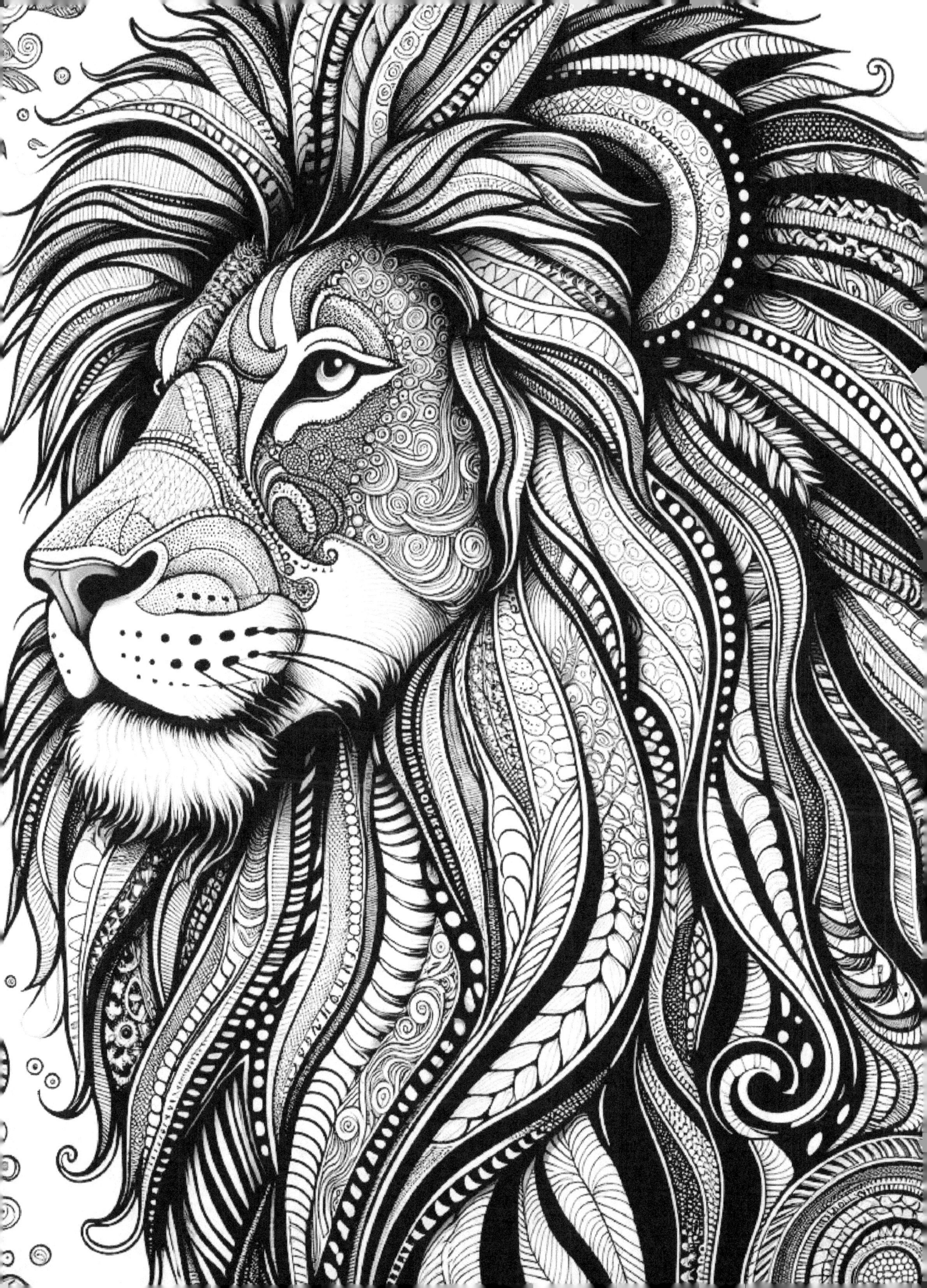

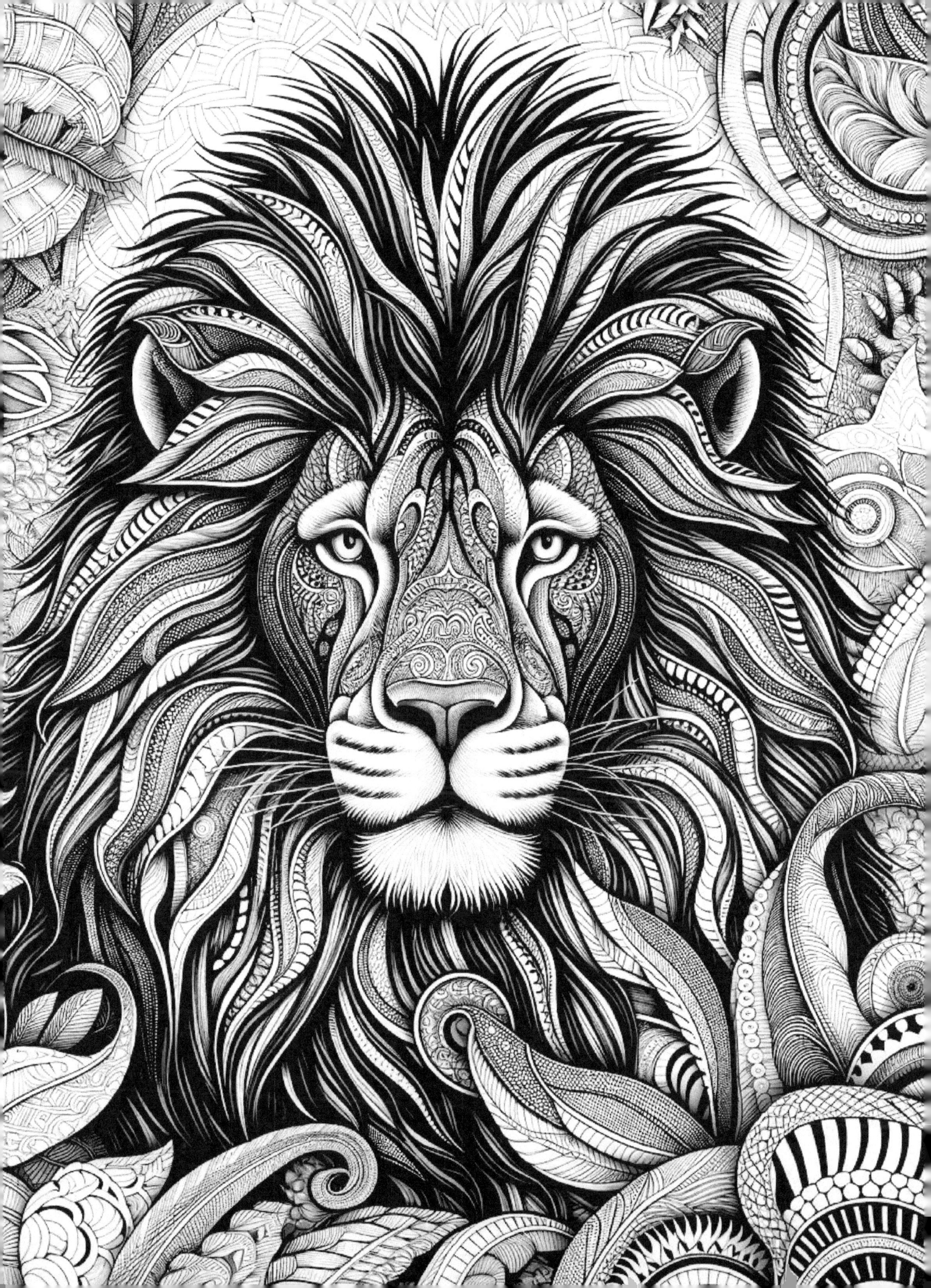

Thank you for joining us on this artistic journey through the world of lions. We hope "Majestic Lions: A Stress-Relieving Coloring Book for Adults" has provided you with moments of tranquility, creativity, and joy. Each lion you have colored represents not just a finished piece of art, but also the calming and meditative experience of its creation.

Keep this book close for those times when you need a break from the hectic pace of life. Let it remind you of the strength and beauty within you, just as the lions do. We encourage you to continue exploring your creativity and finding peace in the simple act of coloring.

Until next time, may the majestic spirit of the lion inspire you and bring serenity to your heart.

www.ingramcontent.com/pod-product-compliance
Lightning Source LLC
Chambersburg PA
CBHW082218220526
45470CB00010B/3224